# 1,000,000 Books

are available to read at

www.ForgottenBooks.com

Read online
Download PDF
Purchase in print

ISBN 978-1-331-85884-3
PIBN 10243088

This book is a reproduction of an important historical work. Forgotten Books uses state-of-the-art technology to digitally reconstruct the work, preserving the original format whilst repairing imperfections present in the aged copy. In rare cases, an imperfection in the original, such as a blemish or missing page, may be replicated in our edition. We do, however, repair the vast majority of imperfections successfully; any imperfections that remain are intentionally left to preserve the state of such historical works.

Forgotten Books is a registered trademark of FB &c Ltd.
Copyright © 2018 FB &c Ltd.
FB &c Ltd, Dalton House, 60 Windsor Avenue, London, SW19 2RR.
Company number 08720141. Registered in England and Wales.

For support please visit www.forgottenbooks.com

# 1 MONTH OF FREE READING

at

www.ForgottenBooks.com

By purchasing this book you are eligible for one month membership to ForgottenBooks.com, giving you unlimited access to our entire collection of over 1,000,000 titles via our web site and mobile apps.

To claim your free month visit:
www.forgottenbooks.com/free243088

\* Offer is valid for 45 days from date of purchase. Terms and conditions apply.

English
Français
Deutsche
Italiano
Español
Português

# www.forgottenbooks.com

**Mythology** Photography **Fiction** Fishing Christianity **Art** Cooking Essays **Buddhism** Freemasonry Medicine **Biology** Music **Ancient Egypt** Evolution Carpentry Physics Dance Geology **Mathematics** Fitness Shakespeare **Folklore** Yoga Marketing **Confidence** Immortality Biographies Poetry **Psychology** Witchcraft Electronics Chemistry History **Law** Accounting **Philosophy** Anthropology Alchemy Drama Quantum Mechanics Atheism Sexual Health **Ancient History Entrepreneurship** Languages Sport Paleontology Needlework Islam **Metaphysics** Investment Archaeology Parenting Statistics Criminology **Motivational**

UNIV. OF
CALIFORNIA

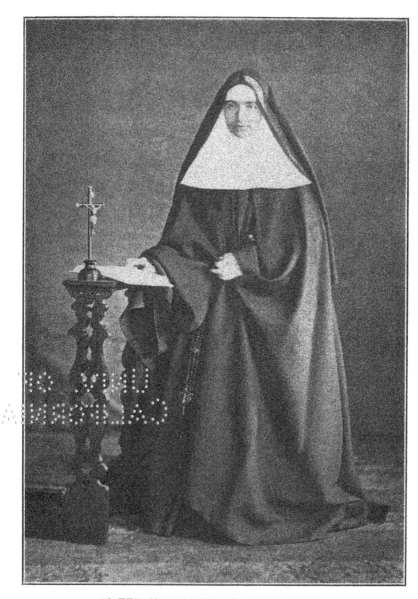

SISTER MARY PAUL OF THE CROSS.

*Life of*

# SISTER MARY PAUL OF THE CROSS

### MEMBER OF THE ORDER OF ST. URSULA
### CONGREGATION OF PARIS

With an Introduction by the

### REV. FATHER XAVIER SUTTON, C. P.

#### OF PASSIONIST MONASTERY,
#### DUNKIRK, N. Y.

URSULINE MOTTO:
*"Sic Luceat Lux Vestra."*

1917

The James H. Barry Co.
San Francisco

NIHIL OBSTAT:
    REV. C. R. BASCHAB, Ph. D.,
                                         Censor Deputatus.

IMPRIMATUR:
    MOST REVEREND EDWARD J. HANNA, D. D.,
                        Archbishop of San Francisco, Cal.

Mar. 25, 1917.

TO THE
BELOVED FAMILY AND FRIENDS
OF
SISTER MARY PAUL OF THE CROSS
THIS VOLUME IS
AFFECTIONATELY DEDICATED.

## PREFACE.

In the life of individuals—no matter how lowly their position in society may be—there are incidents that would interest and edify, if they were only known; for there often arise events that call forth the heroic and sublime in each one's life.

In the life of a religious, therefore, we find in richer and greater abundance, things to interest and instruct; especially will this be realized in the life of one whose duty it was in the capacity of teacher not only to train the mind but also to mold the heart in the love of the highest and the best.

Sister Mary Paul left the impress of her noble life upon all who came under her influence. Those who knew her, do not need a written life to keep alive the memory of her beautiful deeds—she lives in their hearts by the love they all bear to her. Those who did not have a personal acquaintance with her, will find in these pages lessons of encouragement to do and to dare noble and good deeds in their own sphere of life.

She has left:

> Footprints, that perhaps another
> Sailing o'er life's solemn main,
> A forlorn and shipwrecked brother,
> Seeing, shall take heart again.

*REV. XAVIER SUTTON, C.P.*

Dunkirk, New York.

Feast of St. Paul of the Cross,
    April 28, 1917.

## CONTENTS.

### CHAPTER I.

Page

Causes of Emigration of Irish People.—Patrick Morrissey and Family Are Among the Exiles.—Sketch of Patrick Morrissey's Early Life.—Death of Little James Morrissey.—Holy Innocents of Ireland, Famine, Emigration, and Pestilence. . . . . . 13

### CHAPTER II.

Mr. Morrissey and Family Arrive in America.—He Settles in New York.—He Finds Employment in the Erie Railroad Company.—Margaret's Birth, Baptism, and Childhood.—Family Move to Sheridan Center.—The Household of Mrs. Morrissey.—Margaret's Early School Life.—Her Love for the Land of Her Fathers.—Her Attention to Religious Duties.—An Incident Showing Margaret's Obedience.—Isabella of France.—First Communion Day.—Conversation Between Patrick and Sarah Morrissey.—Further Characteristics of Margaret's Conduct Towards Companions and Teachers. . . . . . . . . . . 17

### CHAPTER III.

Death of Mr. Morrissey and Grief of Family.—Margaret's Determination to Help Her Mother.—Letter Written Some Years Later, Bearing on Her Father's Death.—Patrick Morrissey, Brother of Margaret, Is Given Position by the Erie Company and His Success.—Her Devotion on Free Days.—Her Vocation Develops and She Is Directed to the Ursulines of St. Martins, Brown County, Ohio.—Parting With Her Family, and Description of Her Trip to St Martins. 28

## CONTENTS OF PART II.

### CHAPTER IV.

Page

Margaret Arrives at Convent.—Her Meeting With Superiors and Novice-Mistress.—First Weeks of Postulation.—Letter to Sisters in London, Ohio.—First Letter to Her Home.—Mother Chatfield's Tomb.—Sketch of the Life of Mother Julia Chatfield. . . 39

### CHAPTER V.

A Short Sketch of St. Angela Merici, Foundress of the Ursuline Order.—Margaret's Spirit of Penance.—Second Letter to Sisters in London.—Impressions of Daily Life of Novices.—Margaret's Joy at Her Coming Reception.—Preparation.—Her Clothing. . . 51

### CHAPTER VI.

Margaret's New Name.—Her Visits to the Blessed Sacrament.—Manifestation of Conscience.—Studies.—Her Views on Vows.—Exactness.—Retreats.—Profession.—Sent in the Second Band of Sisters to the California Foundation.—Description of Trip Westward to Santa Rosa. . . . . . . . . . . . 58

## CONTENTS OF PART III.

### CHAPTER VII.

Page

Rev. J. M. Conway Obtains Permission from Most Reverend Archbishop Alemany for Sisters to Come to Santa Rosa, California.—The St. Martin's Community Are Asked to Furnish a Band of Sisters for the Enterprise.—Purchase of Christian College (Campbellite).—Ursulines Leave for the Scene of Their Future Labors.—They Are Met in Reno by the Very Reverend Vicar General, J. J. Prendergast, D. D., and by General William Stark Rosecrans and Mrs. Rosencrans.—Letter.—Notice of the Death of Sister Liguori, One of Santa Rosa Pioneer Ursulines, Which Occurred in 1916.—Privations, Incident on Foundations Generally, and on Santa Rosa's Particularly.—Some of the Sisters Return to Ohio, While Seven Remain.—Sister M. Paul's Work and Success.—Her Desire to Dedicate to God Whatever Was Most Excellent.—Her Manner of Correlating Secular and Religious Studies.—Foundation Stones.—Literary Work for Novices and Graduates.—Midnight Incident. 75

### CHAPTER VIII.

Failing Health of Rev. J. M. Conway.—Rev. J. M. Cassin Supersedes as Pastor.—Mother Alphonsus' Death.—Friendships.—Elections.—Particular Virtues of Sister M. Paul at This Phase of Her Life.—Her Desire That Amusing Changes Be Planned for the Young.—Her Appreciation of Napa Valley.—Lines on Its Beauty.—Coming Elections and Sunday School at Sebastopol.—Miss R's. Character Sketch of Sister M. Paul.—Elections.—Picnics.—Letters.—Mrs. Morrissey's Demise, and Clippings Concerning Same.—Earthquake of 1906.—More Letters. . . . . . . . 96

## CHAPTER IX.

Silver Jubilee of Sister M. Paul.—Request of Her Family Granted.—Trip to Dunkirk, New York, and Other Places En Route.—Stay at the Monastery of Quebec; Mother St. Croix Holmes.—Letters. . . . . 127

## CHAPTER X.

Journey Homeward Over Canadian Pacific Road.—Poem on the Rockies.—Stroke of Apoplexy Warns Sister M. Paul of Death.—Mother Angela Elected Superioress.—Final Retreat of Sister M. Paul in June, 1912.—The Manner in Which She Made It.—Sister M. Paul Is Again Sent to Elmhurst Ursuline Academy, St. Helena, on the Opening of New Term.—Her Work Among the Children There. . . . 140

## CHAPTER XI.

Her Death; It Comes at the End of a "Perfect Day." Her Interment in Santa Rosa.—Poem, Testimonials, and Newspaper Obituaries.—Letters. . . . . 149

# Life of Sister M. Paul Morrissey

## CHAPTER I.

Before touching on the life of this holy Religious, our readers may be interested in learning why the United States, not Ireland, is her debtor.

Prior to the immigration of the Morrissey family to New York, Ireland was in the throes of conflicting religious, political, and commercial agonies, which even the genius of O'Connell could not heal; nor could he dispel the deepening gloom which had hung over her for so long. Finally, the entire failure of the potato crop filled Ireland's measure of woe.

It was then that gaunt Famine stalked through the land, striking down first the frail and sickly, then the stalwart and brave. In his wake strode Pestilence, attacking in his turn those who had survived Famine; and so devastating and deadly was their work, that the sufferers could say that

"God Himself scarce seemed there to be."

But, it will be asked, was there need that these tremendous sacrifices be offered daily on the altars of Famine and Pestilence? Was not the ubiquitous soup-house open, with its savory invitation to enter, recant, eat? Verily, and this would defeat the gaunt invader; but where would be heaven's martyrs? Where would be old Erin, in her rôle of Apostolic

Nation, kindling to the uttermost ends of the earth the fire of Patrick's Faith? And, as the sun of England never sets on her temporal conquests, so the sun of her victim sets not on her spiritual ones.

What a heritage this, for Sister M. Paul, a legatee of Irish martyrs! How well she used her inheritance, and at what rate of interest she invested it, let thousands who used her holy income, answer.

In those days men went down to the sea in ships; in those days an Abrahamic call was loudly heard in the land; in those days tiny hands were stretched forth for bread, but received it not; in those days, America, like a new Canaan, was beckoning suffering Erin to her bosom, saying:

"Behold my good, great land, flowing with milk and honey; behold these forests and prairies, these teeming rivers and lakes, these mines and industries, a land in which religious intolerance will not rack the bodies and souls of men."

Answering the call, went forth Erin's hapless sons and daughters, counting among their number many, who, like Eleazar, preferred death, if needs must be, to the eating of illegal meats; who preferred to brave the pestilential ship to the alternative of leaving to the young an example of apostacy. Were not angels' pens kept busy then?—recording the deeds of heroes in heaven's chancery to be kept until the doom.

Reaching the great West, the patience of the exiles in long-suffering was so rewarded that sickness and want were soon forgotten in radiant health and abundance.

To what extent Patrick Morrissey and his young family were affected by the prevailing conditions of his sad country, we cannot accurately tell; suffice it to say, that the March of 1849, found him with his wife and children aboard—not a fine modern scorner of winds, equipped with traveling comforts—but one of the slow wind-driven sailing vessels, ancestors to our astonishing progeny of steam and electricity.

The history of Patrick Morrissey which has reached us, is scant. In 1846, he married Miss Sarah Nugent of his native Clare: and his was one of those marriages, of which it may be truly said that God had joined them, as the subsequent history of their peaceful union endorses; for come weal or come woe, Patrick and his brave wife were ever the same God-fearing couple. Sarah was, as the good wife should be in the order of nature and grace, a complement rounding out the character of her husband. When this sorely-tried family embarked for the New World, they did not leave all crosses behind, for ship-fever broke out among the passengers, and one of the first of its victims to be consigned to a watery grave, was the darling of his parents, little James.

We need not dwell upon the harrowing scene, nor the anguish of the bereaved parents. Judea is not the only place where evil law-givers have triumphed; neither is it the only country blessed by Holy Innocents; nor is Herod the only executioner of hapless infancy. Little James Morrissey, with many of Ireland's Holy Innocents, sleeps beneath the waters that divide the Old World from the New: and numbers testify to what extent Ireland has sent to God her children: nor does the Atlantic, in swaying rhythm, cease the lullaby to their eternal sleep.

When Famine threatened, England might have said: "Be not afraid, O Erin, my sister, though your potato crop is about to fail, you have other crops as rich and nourishing: you have fine herds of cattle and sheep; you have hogs and poultry. Eat and be strong. You want not alms. Open up your own domestic parliament, open your ports to foreign supplies; stop floating off on every tide from your thirteen seaports, your native produce."

But because no blessed Church of God guided the existing Government, the quickly made grave closed over the horrible sight of three million of Ireland's children, dead by starvation or by typhus induced by it, and when the fearful "bad times" were fully, spent, the recording angel had laid at the foot of God's throne his statistics; namely, four million of holy ones lost to Erin by starvation and emigration.

Monuments mark spots in Canada and elsewhere, beneath which lie the hapless victims of fever-reeking ships, who died by hundreds, unable to proceed further from hunger and disease.

# CHAPTER II.

Without further mishap, Mr. Morrissey and family reached Quebec, where after visiting relatives and friends, they set out for New York, which seemed more to their liking than did the Queen's Dominion.

Great Valley in Cattaraugus county offered some inducements to the exile, and it was here that Mr. Morrissey and family settled. Brought to the notice of certain of the Erie Railroad Company, Mr. Morrissey became associated with them and he soon gained their confidence and respect. His ability and integrity were of much use to the company, who were then constructing the Erie Railroad from New York to Dunkirk, and the Morrisseys, who for so long a time had been dwelling on the mountain of self-denial, now began to dig out the gold of happiness and prosperity. Not only to the company that employed him, did Mr. Morrissey give satisfaction but also to those men over whom he was placed. To the latter he was an example of sobriety, industry, and peace; for the good ruler of a family is ever the good ruler of those who elsewhere come under his dominion. No wonder that members of the Morrissey family looked with straining eyes to the evening return of such a father, and he with no less pleasurable anticipations sought them.

Thus was Divine Foresight shaping things for the training and development of a soul over whom the plastic fingers of the Creator soon should wander, that it might come forth therefrom blessed and finished to ornament in due season His Church.

In February, 1856, Mrs. Morrissey's fifth and most favored child was born. The hardihood and development of the mother had not been decreased by the icy, cold, and bitter squalls of old Erie. The Morrissey endurance was of that strong, wiry constituency peculiar to the mighty Celts who were almost in the van of Europe's barbaric invaders.

Great was the joy of husband and family when the waters of Baptism cleansed their little treasure from original sin. This Sacrament was administered on the fourth day after birth, for the pious parents would brook no unnecessary delay in making their child one of God's loveliest and purest.

Margaret Catherine was the sweet name the little one received and let us say that its significance lost nothing of its beauty in the life of her, who was so pure a pearl.

Soon after Mr. Morrissey's business made it necessary to live at Sheridan Center; and the thought of returning to his own land and retaking the fine home of his fathers had to be abandoned; for his affairs were prospering and the building of a comfortable New York home near his work must needs leave the home in Clare out of the question.

In the course of time, other children came, among whom was James, to make good the loss of him who sleeps beneath the Atlantic waves; and Lucy, named after the sweet patroness of the blind, a favorite saint with Margaret and Mrs. Morrissey. In this family was fulfilled the consoling description of the Psalmist, who likens the good wife to a fruitful vine, and the children to young olive plants around the table of the God-fearing parents. These days seem to be the happiest in Sarah Morrissey's married life, and well did she thank God, and prayerfully did she watch over the children whom He had sent for her consolation.

To the casual observer, there was nothing extraordinary about the manner in which the household affairs of the Morrissey family were conducted; yet any one striving after perfection and knowing the difficulties thereof, would find an extraordinary holiness in the day's routine. With the regularity and exactness, Mrs. Morrissey performed her own duties and required the same from her children. The morning and evening prayers, the grace at meals, and the daily rosary were duties from which no one, without a grave excuse, was dispensed. The Sunday Mass, Confession and Holy Communion lost none of their unction by the regularity and repetition with which the Mother insisted on their fulfilment.

No wonder the little Margaret in after years was an example to her religious Sisters of those virtues which had been so well instilled into her who, in riper years, never suspected that she was doing aught above her plain duty; nor could she think the shirking of exactitude anything short of sin.

How often in recreation hour, would Sister M. Paul speak of her mother's fervor at the short and simple grace and rosary; or of the care and industry of her "dear, sweet sister Mary" regarding the younger children. To them, Mary was, as they called her, their second mother and how tenderly she filled her self-imposed office was shown by the loving trust they had in her judgment.

Evenings in the Morrissey home, were spent either in preparing lessons for the children or in discussions among their circle of friends, calculated to rouse the interest of Margaret in matters political and historical. O'Connell's skill for agitating rather than for fighting made him champion for all time in the mind of our little Margaret. Thus a love for Ireland's history was fostered around the Morrissey hearth; and Margaret, in common with her brothers and sisters, was proud of her country, its traditions, its glorious title of "Insula Doctorum et Sanctorum"; and above all she gloried in the Faith of her fathers.

Margaret's progress at school was remarkable, especially in mathematics, a subject in which she afterwards excelled. Convent schools, in those days, were rare blessings and generally located in large cities; so that our ambitious little Margaret, together with her parents, was obliged to be content with what the public school offers; and to an upright child like Margaret, home sympathy with the religious instruction she received, somewhat made up for better conditions. "Be noble and the nobility in others will rise to meet your own," was a command in the Morrissey household; and that the nobility in others did meet theirs, was evident, for neighborly intercourse never descended to the ignoble.

The deprivation of the religious school for his children made Mr. Morrissey doubly careful to instill into his family great devotion to the Blessed Virgin Mary, to the Guardian Angels and Saints of God, and in pious practices he was always leader.

When deep snow and ice covered the five long miles that stretched between his home and the Church, he excused neither himself nor family from attending Holy Mass on Sundays and holy days of obligation. Holding the little hands of his children in his brave ones, he did not halt till he led them up near to the "Holy of Holies."

The journey homeward he beguiled with a recapitulation and explanation of the sermon, and thus they became so well instructed that when little Margaret presented herself for remote preparation for First Communion and Confirmation, the presiding priest, Reverend Hugh Barr, C. P., found a soil thoroughly prepared for the growth in holiness which was to follow.

At this tender age of ten, an incident occurred which shows Margaret's obedience and determination.

Some trouble arose between a pupil and the teacher. The parents of the former took the case to court. Witnesses from the school were summoned, among them Margaret. Before taking her testimony, the officer of the law told her to take an oath on the Bible. Margaret refused, whereupon he explained that the oath was necessary. She replied that she would tell the truth, but would not take the oath.

"May I ask your reason?" said the officer.

"Because my father says I am too young to understand what an oath is," said the resolute little witness.

"Are you a Catholic?" said the officer.

"Yes, sir," was the simple reply.

"Well, then, you may be excused from taking the oath," said he, a little amused at the intrepid youngster.

Margaret's devotion for her first reception of the Holy Eucharist, the Sacrament of Love, culminated in a perfect holocaust of self. "To be yours, O dear sweet Lord!" was her heart-song all that day, as her soul floated on an ocean of love; and in the evening, her parents heard her words of enthusiasm and listened to her heart-song.

When the tiny Isabella of France, clothed in robes of State, stood before the last of England's Plantagenets, then in the meridian of his splendid manhood, he asked the princess, "Are you willing, my child, to become queen of England and to marry Richard Plantagenet?"

"I shall be very happy to become queen of England and to marry Richard," said the ten-year-old aspirant to the English throne.

The court smiled at her precociousness, but Richard took the child and pressed her to his royal heart in which he enshrined her for the remainder of his life, while the court, assembled to witness the betrothal, wondered at the serenity of the queen and praised the childish grace and dignity which added luster to infantile royalty.

How often does the court of heaven assemble to witness its King take the hand of a small aspirant to His Heart, to His Throne and to His blessed work: and how often does it wonder at the grace and dignity of the aspiring bride, all glowing with virginal love: all wishing to be one of heaven's queens: all eager to be enshrined forever in the heart of Christ! How He loves to walk among His lilies, culling them when He cannot resist their beauty! Ah me! He delights in prolific gardens, where He finds clusters of rarest qualities, and sweet, small ones to companion the stronger and greater.

The Day of First Holy Communion is often the test as to how parents have sown virtue's seed in the wondrous soil given them by the Maker of all things: for the early season shows forth the springing beauty, or the lurking deformity of human plants, and we can discern how the various weeds, trimmed and beautified by the cultivator, resemble the "gentle race of flowers"; ordinary flowers become rare exotics; and rare exotics superb growths, exhibiting all the possibilities of the species. See the cultivator, Monica, at work; she does not relinquish the pruning shears of admonition, nor the sprinkler of prayer till she sees her obdurate weed attain all floral prerogatives. See also the exotics, Saints Ursula and Agnes: did they not acquire their full growth, their complete development, as exotics?

The Morrisseys were among the best sowers of

virtues' seeds, and their little Margaret's First Communion Day demonstrated how they had worked up the rich and yielding soil of her soul. There was in her nature a characteristic which dominated her all through her life; namely, she kept nothing on her mind, whether of joy or sorrow, that she did not communicate to those in authority, and once communicated she became tranquil.

Hence before retiring on that eventful night, when heaven seemed to have bowed down to her little corner of earth and made her exuberant with those delights which only God's chosen ones know, she sat between father and mother and acquainted them with what our Lord had whispered to her in the morning. Both listened in reverent silence, for the God-fearing parents felt highly favored that a child of theirs should be called into the "hollow places of the rocks" where, undisturbed, she would hold converse with the Lover of her soul. Too full for words, her father stroked her brown hair and her mother's tearful eyes bespoke her emotion. Seeing which, Margaret fondly kissed her parents and bade them, "good-night," feeling rather than hearing their words of approbation and the sweet blessings that fell from their loving eyes and kindly voices.

We can imagine her entreaties that night when she was alone with her angel guardian, for she was ever in the habit of asking him to protect her, to rule her, and to guide her: but on this blessed occasion, she felt the almost sensible assurance that he would not quit his post till he had conducted her safe to her heavenly country.

But Margaret's parents corresponding to grace, like unto the blessed Mother of God, kept what their child had told them, pondering over it in their hearts.

Patrick broke the silence by remarking, "Well, Sarah, St. Paul says: 'Both he that giveth his virgin in marriage doth well: and he that giveth her not, doth better.'"

"These are consoling words," said Sarah, "and proud shall I be, if our Lord calls our dear Margaret to the state of virginity"; whereupon Patrick took from the shelf an old volume and turning over the pages, he said: "We have not much reason to like the opinion of the cruel Saxon: but Saxon saints are different, and this opinion of St. Aedhelm concerning what Margaret has just said, is as fine as if one of our own Irish saints had written it."

"Read it," replied his wife, eagerly, and Patrick read:

"Virginity is gold, celibacy is silver, matrimony is brass. Virginity is riches, celibacy is freedom, matrimony is captivity. Virginity is peace, celibacy is competency, matrimony is poverty. Virginity is a sun, celibacy is a lamp, matrimony is a servant."

"Had I been well read in these beautiful things," said Sarah, "I think I would have done what Margaret thinks of doing."

"And should you not think yourself honored overmuch by being the mother of one of those consecrated virgins, whom St. Paul extols in the passage which I have just read?" said her husband. To this Sarah assented, and it was with full hearts that both knelt before God to pour out the emotions of love and gratitude which the progress of that sweet day had heaped up in their hearts.

About this time the Passionist Fathers of Dunkirk arranged to have Mass celebrated in Sheridan Center on the fifth Sunday of the months having five Sundays: Mr. Morrissey's home was blessed by having the great Mysteries celebrated therein. We can imagine the tender love of his children in decorating the altar and arranging everything connected with the Divine Service. Reverend Hugh Barr, C. P., generally said Mass on these occasions. His attention was centered upon little Margaret and her brother J . . ., for he recognized in them those qualities which give promise of vocations to the religious life. Margaret was directed by him, and through him her attention was turned to the Passionist nuns, whose novitiate is in Italy.

St. Teresa strongly recommended prudent, learned, and far-seeing directors to guide souls to the heights, and had Mr. Morrissey's children continued to be directed by such, we do not hesitate to say that there were four vocations among them; but Margaret's vocation being the strongest, she adhered most tenaciously to the inner call, and her subsequent action realized her fondest hopes. Both school and home duties received a new impulse, and her attention led her to the first place in her class and to the highest respect in the Morrissey household. Perfection is the result of attention to small things, and toward perfection she continually aimed. To her teachers she showed the most respectful deference, which, in later years, she transferred with more loving and reverential intensity to her Superiors. To her school-companions she was ever the kind, considerate friend, who put them forward, keeping herself in the background; yet they found her inexorable regarding faults to which children are unfortunately heirs. To use schoolgirl phraseology, they found her a fierce teller of truth, a fierce defender of justice; and let us add, that the exercise of those virtues sometimes caused fierce, childish troubles. Her methods in matters of justice were all through life most direct and uncompromising. She soared in a region of truth so high, that quibble, prevarication, or even that necessary quality which we call tact, could not follow. Tact was a quality that she labored in vain to weave into the warp and woof of her dealings with humanity, and fortunate was it for her that her life work needed little of the tactician's skill. It was argued that the cultivation of tact would make her more useful to her neighbor, but she had a way of being useful without this kind of human prudence, for true words (being the children of true thought and true thought the offspring of a noble life) gave method and vigor to Margaret's procedure.

## CHAPTER III.

In this work-a-day world of ours, in its apparent greed for riches and honors and in its disregard for the Ten Commandments, we are inclined to think that few of its votaries are living in the fear and love of God.

Not so, for if we look but closely, we shall discover many peaceful Nazareths in which live holy families with Josephs and Marys, close imitators of their great prototypes. Under their rule dwell children patterned after the Child Jesus, and so holy and smooth passes their existence that they do not realize the dread proximity of Calvary and that all who ascend its heights are cross-laden. A Nazareth, in truth, had been the Morrissey home: but swift and sudden were its inmates transported therefrom and placed on Calvary's summit.

Mr. Morrissey, as we have stated, had been in the employ of the Erie Railroad Company, and to it he had given five years of profitable service. In return he had enjoyed the highest confidence and appreciation of the Company. But grim destiny was abroad. On the twenty-ninth of October, 1870, his train was steaming towards Dunkirk: halting at a small station outside the City, Mr. Morrissey saw a friend of his on the platform. He stepped from his coach to greet this friend, and being interested in the conversation that ensued, he did not observe that his train was moving on.

With his wonted agility, he attempted to board the train; but his foot having slipped, he struck his head against the coach, and losing all consciousness, fell to the ground.

In a few moments all was over, and the inscrutible decree of God prevailed. Mrs. Morrissey, little dreaming of catastrophe, together with her children, was preparing for his glad return, which indeed was prompt, but, alas! not glad.

Perhaps nothing shows forth more the beauty of Christianity than the manner in which its followers bear overwhelming grief.

When the first paroxysm of pain was over, Mrs. Morrissey summoned her fortitude, and taking her eight wailing children, she knelt with them before a picture of our Mother of Sorrows and there she offered her own grief with theirs. Long and earnestly did she mingle sobs and prayers, whilst sympathetic friends cared for the dead. From the kneeling group up rose Margaret, the most grief-stricken of all, and dashing away her tears, she clasped her mother about the neck and exclaimed: "Mother, don't cry. I'll work for you instead of father." How this determination was effected, we learn from her subsequent work both as student and teacher. The death of her beloved father was a sorrow, the poignancy of which remained with her till death as the following letter written a month before her demise will show:

"Feast of St. Teresa, October 15, 1912.
"My own beloved ones:

"It seems a long time since I have heard from home, but I hope you are well. Time passes so quickly that soon another Christmas will be present and then I will get my loving Christmas letters from all. Soon also that eternal Christmas will dawn when we will be reunited with our devoted parents. Just two weeks from today will be October twenty-ninth. How well I remember October twenty-ninth, 1870! Our noble father, called so suddenly from his tender, saintly wife and his idolized children. Do you remember our brave brother P . . . . . .?—how at once he took father's place and thus we remained in our home in Sheridan Center, a paradise on earth with our dear saintly mother, its queen. Just think, forty-two years have flown so rapidly, each one of which has been marked with God's special blessings on my loved ones. Courage, my dear people. Continue in your noble life of faith and of hope and of love of God till you hear the Master's call, 'Come and be crowned.'

"No doubt, you are anxious to know how I have been since I got that stroke four years ago. I have enjoyed good health. Of course, the attack weakened my system so that I cannot use my head in constant mental work, without great fatigue, hence I do not accomplish as much teaching as formerly and I rest when tired.

"The shock left me without any painful effects, as is generally the case, so I am 'up and doing'—

no organic trouble whatever, thank God! I owe it to the tenderness of our Heavenly Father and to the prayers of dear Reverend Father C. and the dear members of the community, our esteemed Mother A. leading.

"You, my dear people, have perhaps the most share in my full recovery. May God love and bless you all! Pardon my egotism, but I know you are anxious to learn just how I am.

"The mountain air in St. Helena is most salubrious. We have a large fig tree which yields so abundantly of delicious figs that I wish I could send you some. We have them morning, noon and night—if we want them. Last evening we sent a box of them to Santa Rosa for dear Sister T.'s feast-day. She is one of the Sisters who was anointed the same week that I was, four years ago. Life is a road, long for some, short for others, but for all, no return. Let us love one another. Be kind and tender in all your dealings with your own. The Morrissey family of Sheridan Center owes its fine history of Faith and Hope and Love to the beautiful Rosary recited every night for so many years. Continue to say it daily and have K.'s darlings say it together. It will work wonders in this age of indifference to our holy Faith."

We draw a veil over the family while they were dwellers on Calvary. Mrs. Morrissey had drained her chalice to the dregs and her little ones drank it according to their capacity, but Margaret's great affection and tenderness toward those she loved, caused her to receive a double portion of the bitter draught and to feel most keenly of all the sense of loss.

When the fearful shock had somewhat subsided, both she and the family with extraordinary courage faced again the same problem which had confronted their father on his arrival in the United States, and here again was God directing their destinies for His all-wise ends.

With great generosity came the officials of the road, who placed young Patrick Morrissey, Jr., though a mere boy, in a section of the road that gave lucrative employment to the youthful breadwinner. Possessing integrity and honor in his dealings, charity and kindness towards all, we do not wonder that young Patrick not only reached his father's position but also went ahead so amazingly that he became to the family a second father.

Margaret, true to her word that she would work for her mother, redoubled her energies and began to teach before she had attained the age of sixteen, a phenomenal age for one who must rule the noisy mansion, called the school-house. Nor did the boding tremblers ever learn to trace the day's disaster on Margaret's face; for hers was serene and young even as their own; and if perchance these little students did find her

"Severe in aught, well they knew that
The love [she] bore to learning was the fault."

Her success as a teacher was due, not only to ability and daily preparation but also to her diligence in studying pedagogical methods of the progressive kind. Her fervor at daily Mass and her mile's walk thereto and her attention to patrons of her school, all helped to make her work speed along on prosperous lines.

Those engaged in the profession of teaching discover sooner or later that no forming or informing will ever make two persons alike in thought or power. Among all men "their differences are eternal and irreconcilable even among those born under the same circumstances." So, too, Margaret's intelligence, wandering over her young charges, became convinced that some were "agates and needed polishing; some were oaks, and needed seasoning; some were slate and needed rending; others clay and needed molding." She also felt that each type had its proper place in God's fair world, the finding of which place would make their shining beautiful, but with a beauty consistent with their nature. God, delighting in variety and never tiring His creatures with monotony, had given her these, His children, to study, not only that she might help them to satisfy their natural cravings for mere knowledge, which craving is a concomitant of education, but, also, what is far more important, that she might direct the purposes of life which would be theirs to fulfill in order to be crowned with the blessings which must needs follow. How ardently did she long to have a school in which she could freely exercise her love for God towards His little ones, and how she prayed Him to hasten the time when her dear mother could dispense with her assistance!

Saturdays she spent at home, and her little brother James accompanied her to Mass. The boy-nature in him could not account for his sister's prolonged stay after Mass, nor could her instruction on the holy mysteries, or the utility of prayer reconcile him to penitential aches about the knees and to lengthened inactivity during the early Saturday hours so dear to the school-boy.

Reverend Father Barr, C. P., as we have stated above, showed a lively interest in Margaret's vocation and still urged her to go to Italy to the novitiate of the Passionist nuns. Soon after this, however, the Ursulines of Brown County, Ohio, were brought under Margaret's notice, and after sundry conferences on the exact place and Order to which God seemed to be calling her, she finally decided with the aid of her director to remain in America and to give her life to God among that portion of His children nestled in one of the vast forests of Ohio.

Reverend Father Hugh Barr and others of the Passionist monastery wrote eulogistic letters concerning the young candidate, so that she was promptly and enthusiastically received by the Ursulines of St. Martin's, Brown County, Ohio. Her assistance at home being no longer needed, she, with characteristic speed, commenced preparations to enter on the religious life, and having, at the end of the term, resigned her position in the public school, she applied herself to prayer and to the study of the spirit of St. Angela.

The time of departure was approaching, and as the days were hastening towards the one upon which she must bid adieu to all that she loved on earth, a great wave of desolation swept over her soul, and so strongly did it threaten to overwhelm her that even prayer did not bring her the strength to break down the barrier between nature and grace. In this extremity she conferred with her experienced Father Barr, who questioned, "Does your mother's heart weigh more than your Lord's?" The reply in her heart made her decide at once to sever all the ties that bound her to her mother and her cherished family. She immediately began her personal preparation to go to Brown County. Her intentions she made known only to her Confessor and to her family. On the morning of her departure, she was so joyful that she seemed to forget that this time she would not return at the end of the week. She started for the train without saying "Good-by": then she reflected and returned. Her mother and brother James were to accompany her as far as Dunkirk, at which place they were met by the Rev. Joseph Flanagan, C. P., who remained with them until the train moved from the station. Margaret remained calm until she bade her mother "good-by": then for the first time nature asserted itself and she wept with the anguish of parting from so loved a parent.

Margaret wrote home in her first letter, "I looked from the car window, and when I saw mother's face, I could not refrain from crying, and for a long time I could not regain my self-control."

She was met in Cincinnati by Rev. Alexis Biermier, C. P., who accompanied her to the Convent, where she arrived at seven in the evening. In Margaret's eight-mile drive in the Convent bus, she observed the fine road splendidly paved by the efforts of the pioneer Ursulines. On either side of this road, wild roses and other flowers peculiar to Ohio hedge the way while glints in the forest let in the ruddy light of sunset.

She thus described her impressions:

"A sudden rift in the trees made a fellow passenger exclaim, 'Ah, there's Old Brown!' Looking where his eyes indicated, I beheld the domes of the Convent. A shrill whistle from Dan the driver, a little further travel, and the 'bus' halts at the boarding-house. Dan throws down the mail: another crack of the whip and then on through the Convent grounds. 'Here is Lake Stanislaus!' triumphantly calls out another passenger, well acquainted with the topography of the domain. 'See the girls, leaning on their oars: look at the swans! See them swim! And those beautiful Australian ducks!'

"I admire everything, the arbors, the rolling lawn, the priests' house and the winding driveway. Our conveyance pulls up at the main building and the passengers alight. Another crack of the whip and the bus heads for Fayetteville, where Dan finds surcease from toil till the morrow."

# PART II

## CHAPTER IV.

A holy ardor marked Margaret's swift ascent up the high flight of steps leading to the hall door of the Convent. The portresses were there as was their wont on the arrival of the 'bus. A few moments more and Margaret was welcomed by the Mother Superior, Mother Theresa, and by the Mistress of Novices, Mother Ursula. At this first meeting, mutual love and trust were born, which grew apace with time. Supper over, Margaret with Mother Ursula escorted Rev. Father Biermier to the priests' house, wherein he received genuine French hospitality from Rev. Father Cheymol, the Sisters' Chaplain.

Returning to the parlor, Margaret knelt beside her spiritual Mother and in humble but glowing words thanked her for having received one so unworthy as she deemed herself to be. "To dwell under the same roof with my Lord is my great joy!" she said, "and how I wish to make my life henceforth one grand act of thanksgiving!" Then kissing the hand of her Mistress of Novices, she asked to visit our Lord in His Tabernacle. Once there, how she poured forth her thanks, how she dedicated her future life, and how she spoke of those who mourned her loss!—all this can be imagined by those who knew the fervor of her outpourings of love before our Lord on the Altar. So fervent was she that she heeded not the wonder of art, the beautiful chapel, wherein rested the golden

Tabernacle of the Prisoner of Love. Here the pain of separation and the fatigue of traveling totally vanished; for when she reappeared, so refreshed was she that she seemed like one who had found her true place in the deep security of conventual dwelling: the compass needle of her inclinations had found its polar star and was at rest; hence, no more weary flutterings at the pivot upon which previous resolution had been revolving. Ensuing days unfolded to her how rich was the happiness of a life that was spiritually nourishing so great a number of human beings, the noblest and happiest on earth—human beings, who, bent on perfecting the functions of body and soul to the utmost, were concomitantly obtaining the widest possible influence over others. A strange commonwealth she found, which annihilating self-interest, transfers all energies to the community whose weal is the business of each member.

The first weeks of Margaret's postulation were spent in observing the labyrinthic ways of the building, in becoming acquainted with the daily routine, and in the performance of such duties as candidates are given, the while their gold is being tested in the alembic of spirituality and common sense.

The following letter to her sister Ursulines in London, Ohio, will illustrate both her work and small first trials:

"Dear Sisters:

"Mother says that we novices must take turns in sending to you each day's news, and since my turn comes to-day, I feel myself honored overmuch in being scribe: every twenty-fifth day I presume I shall write, for we are twenty-five novices.

"My Angel,* Sister Antonia, is acquitting herself in my behalf with zeal and discretion; besides she is ingenious in circumventing my mistakes. She has given me 'Tact' as a little virtue to practise; but with all her help, I find myself in trouble enough. As an instance, a few days ago, I went to the Chapel and there before the Blessed Sacrament, I found Sister Bernardine in tears. I went to her and said, 'Crying, Sister? Crying, and the Spouse so near?' Sister gave me an amused though grateful look, but said nothing. I told Sister Antonia what I had done and how Sister Bernardine had said never a word in answer to my sympathy, to which Sister Antonia replied, 'Sister Bernardine has lost a dear friend; and you, without permission, should not speak to the older nuns, nor should you without necessity speak in Chapel.'

"Another cross came later. I have charge of the aquarium. The other night, I filled it with water but I did not notice that I had poured in water above the safety mark for the gold-fish. Next morning, I found the dear little things on the floor quite dead. Hope against hope compelled me to throw the fishes back into the aquarium—but, alas! they sank to the bottom. Forgetting my finely

---

* Angel is a name given to the sister who installs the incoming postulant.

laundered dress, I put my arm up to the shoulder into the water.

"Finally securing the fish; and with sleeves and cape dripping, I took them to their owner, Mother Berchmans. I met her in the children's corridor, and promptly falling on my knees, and still dripping from shoulders and elbows, I accused myself of my carelessness. Then I awaited results. Mother Berchmans said, 'My child, tell your Mistress of Novices what has occurred and she will attend to it.'

"I arose and hastened to Mother's 'cabinet,' where I learned that giving an account of one's faults should not be done in public places. For penance, I was told to take the Life of St. Francis of Assisi to chapel and read his little sermon to the fishes: indeed, the pathetic sight of the little creatures that my carelessness had killed was quite a penance in itself. I resolved to be very careful as to accusing myself in public places and to be more attentive to my charges. Love to all."

Margaret's first letters to her family are most flattering to "Brown County," as the Convent of St. Martin's is sometimes called; especially was she impressed by the culture of the sisters, whom she likened to a congregation of scholars, secluded within their goodly acres with never a thing to bring them into contact with the commonplace. Their dwelling was a seat of learning for young ladies not only of Ohio but also of surrounding States. Even

Europeans and South Americans were among the students.

"Indian summer is making the upper air brilliant with its wealth of crimson, gold, and russet; while gorgeously repeating these tints in the leafy carpets underneath. The soft, dreamy atmosphere and the deep, religious quiet quicken the pulse of body and of soul"—such is some of the description in Margaret's first letters to her expectant mother and sisters.

In another letter, we find her impression of God's Acre wherein lie some of her Ursuline predecessors. She describes this resting place of the dead, the sunniest, sweetest place—quite in keeping with the beautiful lines of Davis:

"Nor sods too deep; but so that the dew,
The matted grass-roots, may trickle through.
Be (their) epitaph writ on (their) country's mind
They served (their) country and loved (their) kind."

"The little head-stones," Margaret wrote, "are as uniform as the dress the sisters wore in life, and like heaven's great cosmopolitan assembly, so seemed these sleepers—French and German, Spanish and Italian, English and Irish, Austrian and American—for these nations had recruited "Old Brown," from their lofty womanhood, and these women in turn, recruited heaven by a still loftier type, sainted womanhood. Larger head-stones mark the resting place of beloved friends: Mrs. Johanna Purcell, mother of the great Metropolitan and Church pioneer of the West, Most Reverend John Baptist Purcell, D. D.; Miss Kate, his sister; beside whom are two vacant places to be occupied later, the one by Father Edward Purcell, brother of the Archbishop, and the other by the great Prelate himself, who whilst yet in life has signified the intention that his mortal remains should lie amidst those of his beloved Ursulines."

Hearing from time to time bits of sweetest history concerning sleepers beneath these humble little head-stones, Margaret was wont to exclaim, "How the mighty ones have fallen!" Indeed, had the royal bard known Christian types of womanhood, his panegyric over them would be scarcely less touching than that uttered over Saul and Jonathan.

At the tomb of Mother Julia Chatfield, Margaret often lingered. The spirit of this noble woman still dominated all. Her example while living, was an incentive to good, as may be seen from the following pages.

Very Reverend James Callaghan, D. D., says of her:

"An English lady by birth, a convert to the faith by the grace of God; a daughter of St. Ursula by her religious profession;—the foundress of a Convent and Academy famed far and wide for the piety and educational ability of its sisterhood, which this great nun trained for their high and holy vocation; a Superioress for thirty years, always fulfilling the command of the Divine Master to His Apostles by being the least among her sisters and the servant of all, Mother Julia Chatfield, whose name is spoken by thousands with a tender veneration which her virtue never failed to inspire, was of the saints of earth. She is numbered with the saints in heaven.

In this broad land the virgins of the sanctuary, now counted by thousands, are the pride and joy of the Catholic Church. By their angelic purity, by their ceaseless charity, by their prayers that burn with the deepest love of God, these cloistered hidden souls make our faith divinely beautiful to men who turn a deaf ear to the word of God. Among these chosen souls, whom God can make by the gift of His graces, so beautiful and strong, having all the traits of the 'valiant woman,' there could be none more dear to God than the venerable and venerated Superioress of the Ursulines of St. Martins, whom God called to her great reward on the Feast of All Souls. It would be no excessive praise to apply to her who wore with honor the religious habit for forty-two years, the words of the Office of a spouse of Christ: 'Many daughters have gathered riches, but thou hast surpassed them all.' The holiness of her life, and the great work which her rare virtues performed cannot be told in words. It is written in more enduring characters in the inexhaustible labors, the patient toil of thirty years; it is inscribed within the walls of the Convent that will perpetuate her praise from year to year in the warm attachment of the family of God, who knew her only by the title of Notre Mère; in the perfect discipline, and the interior spirit which her example breathed into her now sorrow-stricken community; in that strange power which she exercised, so marked, so clearly defined in the Convent of St. Martin's of assimilating to herself every fresh accession and of winning through the virgin family she trained the hearts of the thousands of pupils who bless to-day her sacred memory. The Spirit of God was largely given to her, and the successful work of her life was to impart to her spiritual children the same spirit.

Thirty years ago this good and great nun left the Convent of the Ursulines at Boulogne-sur-mer in France at the invitation of the Archbishop of Cincinnati to build a fair, rich tabernacle to God in a Western wilderness. She was called to a hard and difficult undertaking. But little of wordly assistance could be offered to her, for the then young Bishop of Cincinnati had no wealth to keep pace with his zeal. He was the poorest of the poor. But this faithful nun was filled with the spirit of her vocation; she knew that it was well to be poor for Christ's sake. Like St. Theresa, she and he who had invited her to this new field where the harvest has been so golden, so precious, while they confessed themselves nothing, knew that God and a little human help working with them were everything. The past tells us how abundantly her trust in God has been rewarded. The log-cabin where she built her first cells for the community has long since disappeared. In its place has risen the large, beautiful, spacious Convent and Academy of St. Martins; the wilderness has literally blossomed and bloomed into a garden of roses, which has filled hundreds of homes with the sweet, fragrant odor of Christian piety and knowledge. She and nearly all who shared in her struggles with poverty and in her joy of being made like Him who was poor for the sake of His brethren, have fallen asleep. But before that eternal rest came, God built for Himself through her more grandly and successfully than this humble religious had ever dreamed of. It was God's work: she was the humble, well-chosen instrument, and the work was accomplished. Thirty years of the precious, holy life of Mother Julia was given to the training of her admirable sisterhood and to the education of thousands who bless the day they crossed the threshold of St. Martins; thirty years in the full maturity of her wisdom and of her spiritual strength was the offering that was laid at the feet of Jesus Christ in the silence of that wilderness.

What tongue shall even stammeringly tell the good that others have reaped from that offering? Who will measure the knowledge of God imparted by her, the love of virtue kindled, the sorrows soothed, and the blessings that have streamed from that fountain of piety over a young and tender generation, entrusted by parents to this wise and prudent virgin? God's day alone will reveal all this. We hope to see it in the fulness of His light.

It is a sufficient indication of the merits of Mother Julia to say that she was perfect in the observance of her Rule and in the practice of the spirit of the Institute. The greatest self-denial of religious life is rigid and persevering adherence to the rule of conventual life in all its details. From this, springs the wonderful unity of religious life. It is thus that the actions, habits, and wishes, and the words and works of all are cast in one divine mold. It is the source of that beautiful charity, stronger than any natural love which binds a holy sisterhood together, and which was so deeply impressed by the guidance and example of Mother Julia upon her community.

In Mother Julia, from out the routine and severe simplicity of the common, exact, religious life, there shone forth a rare intelligence, an intensity of charity, and a heavenly form of wisdom, which marks those called to be rulers of as well as examples to their sisterhood.

What shall we say of the external proof of the holiness of her life; namely, her zeal for the welfare of others? In the beautiful institute which she entered in the days of her young womanhood, she found the means of saving souls and of promoting God's glory. Even in the stress of physical suffering, she never flagged or gave herself the slightest release from the work of doing good to others. The vow which she registered to instruct others in the ways of wisdom, was most faithfully fulfilled. On the white, unwritten page of the souls of the pupils of St. Martins, she traced deeply the lessons of the eternal truth by the veneration which her virtue elicited. The career of her pupils through life, while it shows that the seed of knowledge did not dry up and wither in their hearts, at the same time tells how perfectly Mother Julia fulfilled her blessed vocation. To have had such an instructress was a special benediction. How many of them have felt this!

Many a time in the hour of seductive or fierce temptation has the former pupil of St. Martins seen rising before her in fancy's vision, the holy nun who was her mistress in the convent, and the meek reproach or solemn warning which that vision brought, was a saving grace. It was she whose memory threw over all the pupils a network of affection, which seemed to cover and keep them together, no matter how much they might be separated by distance.

No one charged with the government of others possessed a greater power of discerning dispositions and molding characters. She was a wise virgin and of the number of the prudent. She found out natural inclinations, and by her fostering care, they were developed into virtue. She could gently lay hold of every principle of goodness in the soul of a young pupil or novice and give to it by her words and example the strength of endurance.

But the full value of the life of Mother Julia, its sustained consistency, the beauty of holiness that was within, God alone knew, and she wished that God alone should know it. God gave to her four years of suffering before merciful death came, so that the patience of the martyr might complete the work of His grace in her soul.

During that slow, often agonizing approach to the grave, no murmur ever escaped her lips, no shadow of complaint crossed the face of this wise virgin. "Blessed is that servant whom when the Lord shall come he shall find so doing." Over forty years ago the minister of God said to her on the threshold of the sanctuary in the beautiful ritual of the profession of an Ursuline, "Come, Spouse of Christ. Receive the crown which the Lord hath prepared for thee from Eternity." The crown to which she was called, which she seized with more eagerness and love than any queen ever sought earthly diadem, was the crown of self-denial, the crown of sacrifice. Into that pure white crown God wove the red of His Passion. Unstained she wore it for more than forty years. She was thus prepared for the coming of the Heavenly Bridegroom on the day of the week sacred to the Immaculate Heart of Mary, the Patronal Feast of the religious community to which she belonged. Under the patronage of the Immaculate Heart of Mary, she placed the convent she built, and the pious community gathered within its walls. On All Souls' Day, the day on which the whole Church is breathing forth its prayers for the souls of the faithful departed, God lovingly called to Himself this faithful servant. Again she heard the words of consolation spoken by the Master Himself: "Come, Spouse of Christ. Come, thou shalt be crowned; receive the crown of eternal joy, the reward of a life of continuous sacrifice."

On November 4th, 1876, Feast of St. Charles Borromeo, one of the special saintly patrons of the Ursuline Order, the mourning sisters of Mother Julia Chatfield laid to rest the body which had enshrined as pure, as noble a soul as was ever consecrated to God's service by the hand of religion.

Her portion is surely life everlasting.

# CHAPTER V.

Notre Mère, as Mother Julia was fondly called, together with her nine associates, had followed closely in the footprints of St. Angela, the beautiful prototype of Ursulines; and since Margaret was studying the spirit and labors of such saintly women, a word also of the blessed Maid of Desenzano, may not be out of place.

St. Angela of Merici was not only the Morning Star of feminine education but also was she the exemplar of its practical activities.

At Desenzano, Italy, where the holy maiden lived, she gathered around her young girls, her former friends and playmates, whom she trained in the ways of God. They in turn became her coadjutors and continued her glorious work. Their native Italy rang with approval of and astonishment at Angela's grasp of the needs of the time and her efforts in supplying it with an educated womanhood. Out upon the war-racked world, out upon the devastated trail of Louis XII. in his campaign of French domination in Italy, went Angela's counteracting forces to alleviate the horrors along the bloody trail of the ruthless Gaston de Foix—Bayard tells us twenty-two thousand persons, regardless of age or sex, were butchered by the soldiery in Brescia alone.

The holy Maid of Dezenzano, as St. Angela was called, followed up the spoiler and brought consolation to the stricken inhabitants of her native Brescia.

To imitate St. Angela and the many holy predecessors in the Ursuline Order was Margaret's ambition. She longed for the day to come when she would be allowed to go among the children to continue St. Angela's noble work.

Postulants of the Ursuline Order are not admitted to penitential practices; but Margaret, in the secrecy of her cell, was using a sharp discipline, the same she was wont to use in her little dormitory in Sheridan Center. Some misgiving as to whether she should perform this bodily mortification without the sanction of obedience, caused her to seek counsel from the Mistress of Novices. The latter, knowing that in Margaret she was in possession of a golden treasure that must needs be purified from every dross, reproved her severely for her liberty of spirit in this respect and told her to replace the scourge until told to use it under direction. Margaret obeyed with docility and set about her other duties, thinking that perhaps their difficulties would offer some compensation for this deprivation.

Another letter which she sent to the nuns alluded to in a previous letter shows how she tried to secure this compensation:

"Dear Sisters:

"Again my turn veers round to send you a few lines and, I must say, it is a real pleasure. The novices here are queer beings. Do you know that they are as avaricious of hard, uninviting work as people generally are of congenial tasks? To-day we were sent to wash the dishes and what do you think? There was a scramble as to who should secure for her portion of the work the ugly, greasy pots and pans. I entered the lists and won.

"At an early hour this morning, Sister A . . . . . in some mysterious way became cognizant of the fact that there was an unusually big wash. I also happened into the laundry at an early hour and found her in check apron and sabots, her fine white arms careering up and down on the washboard in rhythmic melody while copious perspiration kept up a running accompaniment. I approached her and proffered my services, but I was told I had no permission; so I returned and found a group of other novices laughing, while one was relating some incident evidently amusing. I joined the group and between their fits of mirth I heard the following:

"Very early this morning Sister G . . . . . heard a violent ringing of the front door-bell. Urging her speed to its utmost, she opened the door and there stood John Doolan the foreman.

"'Sister,' he said excitedly. 'Charlie Swan is dead.'

"'Did the priest reach him in time?' inquired Sister G . . . . . . A loud laugh from John brought indignant blood to Sister's cheek, while John between fits of uncontrollable laughter said, 'Sure it would be a quare thing entirely to send Father Cheymol to the poor swan, although some say the crathers can go to some heaven of their own.'

"On the strength of this incident, we obtained recreation, and Sister G . . . . . . was called upon many times during the day to relate her story of Charlie Swan, and (tell it not in Gath), the story lost nothing by reiterations in German, French, and English.

"An ocean of love is ·flowing towards you from here, and since every little helps, I add my tribute, so that each Sister may be as greedy as she chooses in appropriating her share."

Thus in convents, where wordly affairs are absent, little things provoke mirth, and cheerfulness holds sway. To this fact Margaret was keenly alive. She noticed also how innocent scenes threw the charm of uncorrupted life over her youthful co-workers, making their amusements frequent while smoothing the harshness of life. She observed, too, that the ascetic severity practiced in religious communities is so tempered that it never freezes the genial current of God-given mirth and laughter, and who so happy and cheerful as God's saints who possess the sesame of life's full meaning?

Try this sesame, ye who would drink deep of the cup of joy and prove how good a thing it is to serve the Lord your God. From this cup Margaret was daily refreshed while its inebriating effects kept her in perpetual gladness and made her long for the day of her religious clothing. Great was her disappointment, however, when she became aware that she must wait some months for a postulant who entered later than herself, thus avoiding two ceremonies in close sequence. This postponement she bore with her usual serenity, and by prayer and mortification she made herself daily more worthy of the spiritual engagement that she was to contract with her Lord and Spouse.

The novices near whom she sat at table marveled to see that even on Feast-days she seemed never to gratify the palate; nor did she take food for any other purpose than as a means to obtain life's best results, suppressing every craving to the contrary, although when server she was careful to procure for others the best within her reach.

She looked upon her monastic little world as a miniature Utopia; and in later life, when she came in contact with socialists and their theory of community life, she frequently waxed warm on their stupidity, who if they cared to study could see in every monastery a perfect Utopia. Such study would convince her how admirably adapted to the highest ideals are monastic institutions. Should they find therein a healthy severity, they would also find a healthy joy and happiness. Those, who by nature, are inert and tepid would perforce become useful, filling some void in this well organized commonwealth. Here would be grappled the two wonderful problems that stagger human intelligence: "The one, the rhapsody of grace, that makes saints; the other, the dirge of disgrace, that makes sinners."

"Keep your rule, my child, and your rule will keep you," was the counsel which Margaret often received from her holy Mistress of Novices; and the study of the rules helped her over the period of waiting to receive the veil. Margaret's joy was increasing as the period was decreasing. "But," suggested Mother Ursula, "what if you are not received! Had you not better have your trunk in readiness in the event of your being obliged to return home?"

"Mother, I shall never go; for our Lord would not do anything so diametrically opposed to the will of one whom He knows wishes with all her heart to be His alone."

Notwithstanding her brave speech, she redoubled her prayers and austerities and calmly awaited results. Great, therefore, was her happiness when the moment came to make her demands for admission into the Ursuline Order and greater still her joy on hearing, "My child, you have been received into the Community. Come this evening to begin your preparation for the religious clothing."

Money to cover expenses of reception was in Margaret's possession, but this she laid before Mother Ursula with the requests that it might be used for any purpose she wished and that a costume worn by one of her predecessors might be remodeled for herself. She discovered also an old cloak which had belonged to a saintly deceased nun. This mantle she earnestly asked to be given her, for as poverty was to St. Francis a delight, a treasure—to Margaret it seemed not less so.

These matters settled to her satisfaction, she entered on her retreat and three days thereafter, the splendid ceremonial of the Order of St. Ursula was carried out in the chapel, and Margaret, now bearing the name of Sister Mary Paul, arose from the solemn Prostration, which is a closing feature of the ceremony, to embrace her sisters into the company of whom she had sought admission.

# CHAPTER VI.

The Novitiate now began in earnest, and each day Sister Mary Paul, as she will henceforth be called, was becoming more convinced that it was good beyond all else to serve the Lord; and she strove more than ever to live her Ursuline life in all its fulness.

We have said in the early chapters of this biography that the Passionist Order had interested our saintly novice, and now that she bore the name of its holy Founder, St. Paul of the Cross, she took him for her model, and those who worked beside her knew how closely she followed in his footprints. Like Enoch of old, she "walked with God."

It astonished her co-workers to note the number of visits she made daily to our dear Lord in His Tabernacle, especially when they knew that two flights of stairs and long corridors lay between her duties and the chapel and that often only a genuflection and fervent aspiration could be the extent of her visit. Her quickness in these visits was likened to a humming-bird in its darting, carrying back similarly sweet nectar for future life and strength. When told that she was fatiguing herself by so much effort, she would smilingly say,

"He who loves, labors not."

As star differs from star in glory, so likewise novitiate differs from novitiate in the brightness of virtue. It so happened that Sister Mary Paul's lines fell among the brightest of these dove-cots, and as she says in one of her letters, she was profoundly edified by the manner in which her sister-novices vied with one another in the race not only to win heaven, but also the highest heaven.

Over this novitiate, as has been said, presided the saintly Mother Ursula, who for love of her spiritual children and their heaven-directed interests could not be surpassed. Her wise counsel and her vigilance had but one aim, the perfection of the lives committed to her care.

Manifestation of conscience according to the usage of the Ursuline Directory, was practiced by the novices, and whatever abuses concerning this wholesome mortification occurred elsewhere, among Sister Mary Paul's sister novices, it was productive of the highest good. The evening manifestation, preparing as it did for the morrow's Holy Communion, was always a step heavenward, and steadily and surely did it advance the upward journey.

Time was so divided by prayer, study, and manual labor that the best moral, mental, and physical results accrued therefrom and Sister Mary Paul's alacrity along these lines was astonishing and often the theme of pleasant raillery, for frequently she was told by a sister-novice that she should have scruples for flying too fast to her work.

"Dear sister," said the flyer, "I never have time to indulge in the luxury of scruples; I'll leave them to people who have leisure."

Her progress in secular studies kept pace with those of her religious ones. Mathematics and kindred subjects were more to her taste than others, and she often said to literary students, "I am too matter-of-fact for the poetical"; however, she applied herself to the Latin language with great facility; and the poetical works of Horace and Virgil had few keener students. In later life, these subjects were taught by Sister Mary Paul, and priests and professors who attended her examinations complimented her on her excellent methods of presenting the classics to the uninitiated. Even studies for which she had less aptitude received her full attention, whenever obedience charged her with them.

The two retreats made during her noviceship show from her resolution book how much in earnest she was. Regarding the Vow of Poverty she writes, "I must not only be poor in spirit, but also in very deed. If, when supplies are given us, I have choice of two things, I shall always select the inferior, leaving the better article for others who are far more deserving of good things than I," and, in truth, to this resolution she adhered to her death. "I shall not waste time, and for my Patron in this resolution, I now take St. Alphonsus Liguori, from whom I shall try to deserve help." Be it known that St. Alphonsus had taken a vow never to lose time. Those, who for forty years had lived and worked with our saintly sister, testify to her extraordinary attention regarding this resolution, and St. Liguori himself must have seen from heaven what a close competitor he had.

Another of her resolutions was on exactness, in the practice of which she, at the sound of the bell, literally left the "letter unfinished" and hastened to obey. Almost the second stroke of the rising bell throughout her life found her on her knees in fervent communication with her Maker. "Exactness is a kingly virtue," she would say, "and I, who aspire to heaven's queenship, must not be wanting in the King's service," therefore was she an enemy to any loitering of the children after the bell had called them; and many of them in after life felt the benefit of her exact training.

The steps she took in these virtues, she called stitches in the black veil, which she was most eager to see finished and placed on her head. Well and carefully had her black veil been stitched, and by the time the period of novitiate had expired, the veil was indeed prepared, and Sister Mary Paul of the Cross, radiant with hope fulfilled, presented herself with her sisters to enter the remote preparation for Holy Profession. This semi-retreat lasts eight weeks, after which the solemn retreat begins, continuing about ten days, and during this period a novice must study deeply the life she proposes to herself, her duties to the Community, and its duties to her. She must study her calling in its severest requirements to ascertain if she be strong enough in health, will, and affection for the step she is about to take. She is advised not to undertake the life unless the necessary requisites are full and well-grounded; but in the case of our holy novice, nothing could be more in harmnoy with her deep religious nature than the obligations that she was craving to contract; and, in fact, a misgiving regarding her holy vocation did not cross her mind from the moment of her entrance till the moment of her death. Therefore, deep and full was her joy, when she heard the Divine whisper: "Come into a desert place and rest awhile." Eagerly she went and sweetly she rested in the holy exercise of prayer. Her extraordinary correspondence to grace and its inspirations deserved for her those blessed allurements which take the soul into the "Hollow places of the rocks," where, in profound silence, it hears unspeakable things from its Beloved.

In the first week of May, 1881, began the retreat for the solemn profession. During retreat days, mortification and prayer go hand in hand. Little sleep, and much prayer and work, was the routine for the four and twenty hours of each day; but, Sister M. Paul was ever describing herself as living on Thabor from which she would fain not descend.

May 4th having arrived, our fervent novice beheld with joy its dawn.

> "Lo, in the sanctuaried East,
> Day, a dedicated priest
> In all his robes pontifical exprest,
> Lifteth slowly, lifteth sweetly,
> From out its Orient tabernacle drawn,
> Yon orbed sacrament confest,
> Which sprinkles benediction through the dawn."

Such dawning stimulated the fervor and joyful anticipations of the coming nuptials with the Lord of heaven and earth. The world saw Day coming, but only the mystic Bride of Christ could understand his sacerdotal pomp on this occasion. She, who knew her "potential cousinship with mire," knew also that the soul within her was exulting with closer kinship to Christ her Lord. She felt herself, as indeed she was, recreated and placed in a Terrestial Paradise, without even a misgiving of forbidden fruit, serpent, or aught that could cause expulsion therefrom, for she possessed an over-mastering confidence—this child of intense love. "Thou hast constituted me singularly in hope."

Dressing herself with more devotion than ordinary, she was fastening on her girdle when she remarked to the Mistress of Ceremonies, "Earthly bridegrooms encircle their bride's finger with a circlet of gold, but mine places His circlet about the heart, the region of love!" Then she descended to the chapel with holy eagerness, saying, "Soon my hand will clasp His, the hand of my heavenly Spouse in wedlock to unclasp nevermore." O how majestically beautiful is this word "Nevermore" when it excludes all that is opposed to the possession of the Supreme Good!

Eight o'clock May 4th (1881) witnessed the sombre procession of Ursulines, bearing tapers and leading the eager victims to the morning sacrifice. Slowly and solemnly, the priests filed into the chapel and amidst reverential decorum, holy Mass began and continued to the "Domine, non sum dignus," when Sister Mary Paul, the senior of her band, approached the altar, and in the presence of the Blessed Sacrament pronounced the holy Vows of Poverty, Chastity, Obedience and of Employment in the Instruction of Young Girls, commonly called Institute. These, in the secrecy of her heart, she had been pronouncing the greater part of her life.

The Most Reverend Archbishop William Henry Elder, D. D., having received her Vows, invested her with the black veil and presented the Crucifix. Then through the vaulted arches of the chapel rang the glad Te Deum—signal for the newly professed to fall prostrate before the altar and to give themselves up to the solemn thanksgiving of creature to the Creator.

If beauty be the Divine thought of excellence, the last touch on God's handiwork, surely a scene of this kind bears the genuine stamp; for beautiful were the sanctities of flowers strewn by innocent hands over the prone figures before the sanctuary; beautiful the sacerdotal group now completing the functions of their morning office; beautiful the high Priest in glittering vestments; beautiful the sound of instruments and voices of heavenly sweetness attuned to the occasion; beautiful the souls of those who had by their act demonstrated that one moment in the courts of the Lord is better "than thousands in the tabernacles of sinners." For the nonce, Heaven seemed very near the earth, so holy were the feelings which were keeping the souls of the newly professed oblivious to a sinful world, but alive to the blessed soul-state in which they lay prostrate.

The Te Deum ends, and the "Ecce quam bonum" recalls them to the world of sense. Reluctantly they rise, and like the men of Galilee gazing into the blue ether where Christ had just become invisible, the sisters also seemed to hear the Angel of the Ascension assuring them that the Christ whom they had seen, would come again; and if now they must forego His blessed intimacies, yet will He come during prayer and work, during joys and sorrows, during health and sickness. But the "Ecce quam bonum" of the nuns' choir continues to invite them to the strangely-loving exercise of the Ceremonies. Obeying, they are embraced first by the Superioress, then by the members of the Community, after which they retire from the holy place in the manner of their entering, and soon they find themselves in the midst of friends; who some laughing, others weeping, greet them as beings "too pure for the touch of a word."

Doing some violence to herself, Sister M. Paul goes forth for congratulation to the festive board with her friends; but on her way thither, she must pass through gardens, now a scenic splendor of pink and green—the students in their regulation summer costume forming the pink contingent, approach en masse, and circling round her inquire if she were not "Awfully glad that the long retreat was over," and the like. In that arch way of hers, Sister Mary Paul said, "Dear children, if you were sophisticated in retreats or could define their meaning, you would not ask these questions. I advise that you give retreats one good trial; then if you will not secure them at any cost, it will be strange indeed."

In the evening of this auspicious day, the guests among whom was Bishop Toebbe, were entertained by a play and by tableaux representing the martyrdom of St. Ursula and her holy companions.

Thus closed Sister M. Paul's day of days, the day of her "second Baptism," as Profession in the religious life is wont to be called. The spiritual glory of it was climbing to the zenith, losing as it went its scenic splendor to yield place to the sanctities of deep night. The echo of divine songs rings in the little cell wherein Sister Mary Paul may again be alone with her Beloved. She enters fatigued, it may be, in body; but how animating and refreshing to her soul is ever divine converse.

Since in conventual life, its to-morrows are like its to-days and yesterdays, the professed nun finds little difference between her time of probation and that which follows. It is true, the anxiety of uncertainty gives place to certainty and the calmness of security in God's House and in being a member thereof is thankfully felt; yet the life has its ups and downs, its joys and sorrows, and did these not abound in every phase of life, might we not die of inanity? But our lately professed was destined to no such death. She must move in stirring times, for there had been shimmering in the air, more than faint suggestions of a California Ursuline foundation; but little heed gives Sister Mary Paul to things which she says do not concern her.

"Perhaps you might be sent to California in the next band," remarks a young companion. "If I am sent," she replies, "I think I should feel greatly honored that God selected me to do something very hard for Him. Why should I wish to be in one place more than in another—for 'The earth is the Lord's and the fullness thereof.'"

July of this year ushered in the hottest weather ever experienced by even the oldest settlers around Cincinnati. The annual retreat previously arranged was announced, and Rev. Father Brady, S. J., director of the retreat, had arrived in the midst of the overwhelming heat. Rev. Father Cheymol suggested the advisability of postponing the exercises to a cooler period, but Father Brady, with the proverbial obedience of a son of St. Ignatius, replied, "I am sent to conduct this retreat and must begin it this evening," and he added, gravely, "It is better to burn here than hereafter." Accordingly the retreat began and the "desert place," to which retreat is likened, did not belie its full scorching significance. But the beautiful example of the director, his endurance and his love for God which rejoiced at inconvenience, gave so fine an impulse to the exercitants that, when they had finished the retreat, all pronounced it the greatest of their lives.

Sister Mary Paul seemed like one who had been admitted sooner than she had deserved to taste again the ineffable sweetness of close communion with God: she heeded not the great heat even though towels instead of handkerchiefs were used to stem the tide of perspiration. In the free time she prayed on in the chapel, while some sought the woods for coolness, though in vain; for fierce heat invaded even their density precluding the smallest mitigation of discomfort.

Retreat being over, the California foundation cloud shimmered no longer, but burst upon her like a nimbus mass with never a suggestion of silver lining; for Ursulines who scarcely know what parting means, are not only sisters one to another, but also beloved friends whose affections are severely tried by separations.

Among those to be sent to the Golden State was Sister Mary Paul, and though nature was wrenched to its depths, no demur escaped her; on the contrary, a holy joy seemed to take possession of her as she prepared to leave St. Martins on the Feast of St. Mary Magdalene, 1881. Though she had been professed a little over two months, to detachment and its accompanying growth in holiness, she aspired. Accordingly, on the morning of July 22nd, she bade farewell to her beautiful convent home and to its holy inmates, and with Mother Gabriel, Sisters Agatha, St. John and Martina, departed for the far West.

Since God is not outdone in generosity, He made the journey to the "Land of the Setting Sun" full of pleasure. Most congenial to her nature were her four companions, and as the vast forest of the Middle West gradually gave place to the vaster prairies, Sister Mary Paul's parting griefs were yielding place to joys sacred to the friendship of her fellow travellers. Although the poetical in her nature was not of high order, still she was quick to catch the enthusiasm of others. Thus awakened and observing with attention, she could detect the salient points in the astonishing panorama momentarily produced in the wake of the rushing engine; so that her soul was expanding to the wonders of the West, the infinite ocean of grass rippling with wild flowers, upon which no eye save God's or His sinless beasts had ever rested; nor had the fragrance of these regions ever ministered to man's pleasure, yet who shall say these things are wasted? Has not the eternal Father set His Tabernacle in the sun, whence emanates all essence for growth with its manifold requirements, and therefore why should Mother Earth fail to spread out under this His burning tabernacle, the richest of her fragrance and beauty? But the train moves on, tiring enthusiastic eyes with scenic profusion, though their reserve force must soon be summoned for Wyoming and Colorado, land of impenetrable rock-enskied monsters, fantastic, lavish, confused, bewildering, baffling the wildest conception of human builders, suggesting titanic architects, scorners of space, who columned to the clouds and stretched their mighty architrave beyond. No desecrating sounds break the awesome silence, no pontifical pomp hallows these vast cathedrals, no garrison protects these impregnable citadels of the skies—only awe holds sway and sublimity stirs to the nethermost the depths of man's religious nature.

Enthusiasts in sight-seeing were Mr. and Mrs. T— of Montreal en route for Australia. Mr. T—, an Episcopalian Minister, was all that could be desired in an acquaintance of the most refined and manly type. The same prudence and generosity characterized Mrs. T—. Their graciousness so impressed Sister Mary Paul that she kept in her office book pious leaflets which they had given her and which were found there after her death; the fact arguing how prayerfully she remembered friends and acquaintances.

A waning of things gigantic bids our travellers prepare for supper, which they are to have in Salt Lake City. Very soon the train pulls in and a good meal awaits them at a fine hotel, for dining from lunch baskets makes a hot supper both needful and refreshing.

"Do you realize, Sister M. Paul, that you are supping in Brigham Young's stronghold?" said Mother G.

"I do," was the reply, "and I am thinking how the dear Lord must hate polygamy, since on the trail of the Albigensian, He had sent a Dominic; on that of Luther, an Ignatius and an Angela; and in Calvin's wake, a St. Francis de Sales; while so far, no Saint's fiery zeal has followed Brigham Young whose machinations so threaten social order and the dethronement of parental sanctity. 'I shall abandon them to the fury of their passions, I shall send them dogs that will not bite,' in other words, a useless priesthood: this was God's extreme punishment to the Jews when their sinful excesses went beyond punishment by war and pestilence. In like manner, polygamy has even now a dead conscience and a consequent withdrawal of God's grace."

Leaving Salt Lake City, the Sisters arrived at Truckee, where in the early morning two clergymen

# Life of Sister Mary Paul of the Cross

entered the car. The pleasant "Welcome, Ursuline Sisters," of Rev. Father McNally was gratefully acknowledged by Sister M. Paul and her sisters. Then the ascetic-looking Rev. J. M. Conway with growing warmth, shook the hands of his future co-workers, and gave his "Cead Mila Failthe." Seeing a somewhat meager breakfast spread before the sisters, the priests stepped from the car and soon returned with specimens of California fruits. Flight of time was scarcely noticed in so good and enthusiastic a company, till "Oakland" was shouted by the brakeman, and with the usual rush the overland train set down the tired passengers safe and sound.

At the service of the sisters was a carriage for the day, the kind forethought of Mrs. Peter Donahue; but the north bound train to Santa Rosa gave no time for driving, so with a hasty glance at the Queen City of the Pacific, the travellers bade adieu to Rev. Father McNally and were presently en route for the City of Roses wherein the first band sent out from St. Martins had already resided one year. Arriving at the Convent, the joy of reunion can better be imagined than described.

# PART III

UNIV. OF
CALIFORNIA

Entrance to Grounds

## CHAPTER VII.

It was in the summer of 1880 that Reverend J. M. Conway, pastor of St. Rose's church, Santa Rosa, California, obtained permission from the venerable Archbishop Alemany of San Francisco to invite the Ursulines of St. Martins, Brown County, Ohio, to found a parish and boarding-school. His Grace having heartily acceded to the request and the beautiful Sonoma Valley offering every advantage for successful school-work, Santa Rosa became the first home for Ursulines on the Pacific Coast.

A commodious building, used prior to the event for a Campbellite College, with five acres surrounding it, was offered for sale. Mother Berchmans O'Connor, a woman of superior business attainments, and the young and ardent Sister Alphonsus Costello, were sent to make the purchase, should they find it suitable. Seeing that all promised entire satisfaction, they bought the property, and being invested with plenipotentiary powers, they concurred with Reverend Father Conway to move the parish church from Fifth Street to the Convent grounds. The land for this purpose they donated to the parish, thus safeguarding in the proximity of the church the rule of cloister. The new site being more central, was eminently pleasing to the people both for services and Sunday-school purposes.

When these negotiations were completed, the Community in Ohio was requested to send at once the Sisters intended for the foundation. The patronal feast of St. Ursula was near, the last which the sisters would spend together. It was a day of mingled joy and sorrow, for as we have said, the Ursulines of Brown County were bound by ties of all that was sisterly in the tenderest acceptation of the word.

At this date there was no indication that Sister M. Paul would ever see the Golden West, and yet she was destined to bear its heats and colds, and later to enjoy the success there to be achieved. As has been already stated, Sister Mary Paul was one of the second band.

St. Ursula's Feast being over, the next day, October 22, 1880, there started for the West, Mother Xavier Carolan, as Superioress, with her co-laborers Sisters Liguori Hammer, Sister Kostka Rosecrans, Sister Helena Hines, Sister Michael Kelly, two novices, Sisters Vincent Dooher and Genevieve Lenehan, and Miss Anna Gallagher, a postulant.

Through conflicting emotions of zeal for the undertaken work and of memories of the dearly loved home, they arrived safe on October 28th. Very Reverend J. J. Prendergast, D. D., Vicar-General, with General and Mrs. Rosecrans, met the party at Reno and received them with every mark of respect, esteem, and genuine welcome. Tarrying a few days in the City of St. Francis, they finally, on the vigil of All Saints, reached their new home and in a few days were prepared to begin work in the Parochial School.

Over a hundred eager faces were scanning the future teachers, as Mother Xavier was making, what might be termed, her inaugural address. The Reverend Pastor's zeal urged him also to make some remarks on the auspicious occasion. Thus was the good seed put into the ground, whose later sprouting and growing gave promise of a rich harvest; such the school and community that welcomed Sister Mary Paul and her four companions the following year.

We are too close to experiences to detail them in their true light, but a future pen, no doubt, will do justice to this Santa Rosa Ursuline Foundation theme. Suffice it now to quote a letter from Sister Liguori to Mother Theresa, which will speak in the sense:

"'Ab uno, disce omnes.'

"Santa Rosa, Cal., November 14, 1880.

"My very dear Mother:

"Your kind sweet letters were duly received, and it is really a shame to keep you waiting so long. But it was an utter impossibility for me to write sooner. We had so much house-cleaning, scrubbing, and the like to do. Of course, I as senior member of the Community, pitched in with heroic enthusiasm! My skill in the art of scrubbing was highly admired by the dear kind novices, and they are truly generous and noble; but it would have been far more advisable for me to have taken a few practical sweeping and scrubbing lessons before my departure to the scene of action, than to have learned gold-work . . .

"The house was in a frightful state of disorder, and even now it is not much better, although we are doing our best to introduce order.

"Last Monday, November 8th, we opened our schools; namely, Select School for Girls, Parish School for Girls, and Parish School for Boys. I shall help the younger sisters in their appointments to the best of my abilities.

"The climate is mild and beautiful, but the mornings and evenings are cold. The stars are magnificent, owing to the clearness of the atmosphere. I enjoyed the trip very much. The majestic, awe-inspiring scenery of the Rocky Mountains was a source of infinite pleasure. Every faculty of mind and soul was deluged with intense delight. If I only had had time to study these rocky tablets of prehistoric ages more at leisure! How wonderful are the works of creation!

"I was perfectly well during the journey, and I did not suffer from cold hands or feet. But all my tribulations began at San Francisco. I must postpone this chapter of woes to some future period. I am still suffering from the effects of scrubbing and window-washing. The dust is 'perfectly awful' and the flies are of gigantic size and exceedingly impudent. They have not the slightest regard for 'Her German Highness.'

"Dear Mother, please tell Sister Josephine that it is impossible to write her just now, but I hope I shall soon be able to keep my promise. I delivered her message to Rev. Father Conway. He seemed much pleased when I told him how zealously dear Mother Josephine had worked for the California foundation, and he said that he would write her. Viewing matters from my standpoint, I think dear Sister Josephine has reasons to thank God that she is still in dear Brown County. Our present mode of life would scarcely suit her. Since November 2nd, I have not spoken to Rev. Father Conway except in the Confessional, rather behind an old table where we kneel to make our confessions. At some future period, I hope to be able to write a more detailed account of my experiences in California, and I think Robinson Crusoe will be totally eclipsed. My hands are truly in a pitiful condition, and the prospect for their immediate future is darker still. Until the present, dear Mother Berchmans took charge of the wood-pile, but I think that interesting duty is to devolve upon me. My personal appearance resembles dear Sister Martina when she is cleaning the furnaces. Such transcendental miseries are more than a psychological enigma to my aesthetical nature. Oh, if I could only keep clean! Oceans of dust everywhere! I have so much work; and we are so very poor that I think Mother Xavier will scruple a stamp: therefore, I thank each dear sister not only individually but also from force of circumstances collectively, for the manifold acts of kindness and sisterly affection of which on their part I have been recipient. Tell Sister Ambrose that I am still using one of her little tin cups as a goblet and tooth mug, but have hopes that after Mother Berchmans' departure I shall get her jelly-glass, though somewhat defective.

"Say to dear Mother Assistant that I shall consider it one of my duties to keep her posted in regard to the statistics of the school.

"I think that the California climate will suit my constitution, but I can not say the same for my present mode of life. Supernaturally speaking, however, I am full of peace, joy, consolation, and hope, and God is certainly propitious toward me. I recommend myself to public and private prayers.

"With love, I remain

"Your devoted sister,

"SISTER LIGUORI."

This most noble woman afterwards returned to Brown County. She passed to her reward February 27, 1916. The following clipping from the Catholic "Telegraph" will doubtless be all that those outside convent precincts will know concerning her most useful life, her unusual gifts of mind, and her simple childlike virtues, for earth's greatest have in them a sort of perennial childhood. The clipping reads as follows:

"Deep grief afflicted the Ursuline Community, McMillan Street, Cincinnati, Ohio, when death came to Sister Mary Liguori Hammer on Sunday after a brief illness. Sister Liguori, who is a sister of Rev. Bonaventure Hammer, O. F. M., of Lafayette, Indiana, well known in Cincinnati, had been the teacher of philosophy at the Cincinnati Academy, and her beautiful life endeared her not only to her sisters in religion but also to the many friends she made during her residence in this city. She was a woman of deep learning, a zealous worker, and a devout nun. The influence of her estimable character and the effect of her scholarly teachings have left their impress upon hundreds of pupils who passed from under her charge.

"Sister Liguori was a native of Karlsruhe, Germany, and was in her eightieth year when death overtook her. She came to this country at the age of twelve in 1861, imbued with religious fervor, and dedicated her services to the cause of religion. The greater part of her religous life was spent at the Brown County Academy, where she taught until she took up her position of teacher of philosophy in the Ursuline Cincinnati Academy. The loss of so learned and so efficient a teacher will be greatly felt by the local community, and her demise will be sincerely mourned by the alumnae of the academy of whom she had made fast friends.

"The funeral Mass was sung on Tuesday morning by Rev. A. C. Adelman. Rev. Antonine Brockhuis, O. F. M., pastor of St. George's Church, preached the sermon, lauding the beautiful religious character and sterling qualities that shone forth in the life of the deceased. R. I. P."

Although Mother Liguori's pen gives a humorous turn to the privations endured by the Ursuline pioneers of Santa Rosa, nevertheless, they were privations which were sternly felt; but in the sweet serene nuns that moved amongst the pupils, no trace of meager living could be detected; for was not one aware that her Heavenly Father knew that she "had need of all these things"? and little by little the fiber of those who endured, became so well seasoned that it firmly withstood all shock of passing discomfort. Daily they were climbing Sinais, but too humble to know it. Their souls heard only the Voice uttering the saving Ten Commandments and the call to perfection; and they thought only of rehearsing the same tenets to the dwellers on the plains, lest the golden calf of human passion should find worshipers there.

Another cause of anxiety in those days was the approaching elections. Among trying experiences of community life is the change of the officials. Periods of three or six years find convents under a new régime, and a Superioress whose natural and religious character has won the affection and esteem of all, must, when her term of office expires, give place to the newly elected whose ruling qualities are a terra incognita to those over whom she is to be placed. Nevertheless, each incoming Superioress leaving her impress on her period of government, sameness is prevented. It is noteworthy also that Superiors of convents are proverbial for their business abilities; while the economy which the vow of poverty enforces, helps their achievements. "It is a mystery to me," said a University Professor to the writer, "how Convent folk are able to erect such fine buildings on incomes so slender." Alas! little is known of the sacrifices that uprear these structures; but the history of various monastic institutions demonstrates that strong faith coupled with splendid idealism and hard work have accomplished wonders in religious houses. How many valiant servants of God have started work with a capital of five dollars, or even less; yea God's Providence has been the sole capital of some who are now succoring thousands in comfortable dwellings, while God, their unfailing banker, prevents bankruptcy.

Thus these heaven-sent religious Superiors watch over the economics of their miniature republics and prove, if outsiders care to study monastic sociology, that the best government is one which is not felt; that

Class Rooms
Chapel and
Tennis Court

Entrance to
Class Rooms

TO MIMI
AFFETTUOSO

the best government produces the happiest people and the highest types of the race. Could these conditions be realized in even one commonwealth, gubernatorial skill would reach its height and would possess the secret of human contentment in ideal ruling.

In the Santa Rosa foundation, vicissitudes of varying kinds form some of its early history. The number of boarders was two from Tiburon, aged respectively nine and seven. The revenue for the house expenses must come through the boarding-school, and in default of this the work cannot progress. To leave nothing undone that could make the new foundation a success, the staff of teachers sent to California were women of extraordinary learning and accomplishments, determined moreover to make their western home as famous as their eastern one; but alas! the forty boarders promised in good faith before the sisters left Brown County were represented by two, as already stated. Bravely, however, the sisters struggled on. Seeing no prospect of increase, the older sisters were recalled, and of the younger, seven were allowed to remain with the parochial school. Among the seven was Sister Mary Paul, who found ample opportunities to practice her many virtues even to the third degree. Her uniform cheerfulness buoyed up the others, who were somewhat discouraged under the slow movements of success; while her redoubled fervor secured many graces and blessings for the devoted seven who had remained, and who notwithstanding their difficulties were doing splendid work among the children of St. Rose's parish; besides, Rev. Father Conway, perceiving in the band, material that bespoke latent power for all that was worth while, encouraged them to stand bravely to the work of his parish, a work which he said was already progressing beyond his most sanguine expectations. His utmost co-operation was with them.

The next year brought so many children that every available place was filled; and Mother Alphonse, who was the newly-elected Superioress, announced that prayers for boarders should cease till greater accommodations were erected.

Success delayed no longer but came with rapid strides. Sister Mary Paul was appointed Mistress of the Young Ladies, an office which she filled with results that came from the love she bore her dear children; and beautifully trusting were the veneration and affection which she received in return. "Thou shalt love thy neighbor as thy self," was her basic principle in working among children; and who show more readily than they that love begets love?

At this time Sister Mary Paul's teaching was divided between the boarding and parochial school, so that her influence extended to a great number of children. Besides, she had charge of the First Communion class of each succeeding year in the Sunday-school and her love for such labor knew no bounds. So devoted was she in these "holy classes," as she called them, that she had charge of them till her death.

Often after a most fatiguing day, would she devote her little free time in teaching only one child, whose duties would not permit him or her to come at the usual instruction hour. To persons living in the country and places remote from religious influence and lessons, she devoted much of her Sundays. To-day there are scattered over California and elsewhere men and women who are exemplary fathers and mothers, because Sister Mary Paul labored amongst them, loved them in Christ, and forgot herself for them.

"If I am tempted to stay away from Mass on Sunday," said one of these young men, "Sister Mary Paul is almost palpably present to me, urging me to go; should I resist, I feel as if something of evil were about to happen to me."

Letters from her kept the careless from slipping backwards, and lifted the careful to higher planes of sanctity.

She was always eager to examine her classes in presence of the Reverend Pastor, and great was her exultation when she saw the many blushes and rejoicings consequent on his high commendations, uttered in approving voice and generally accompanied by the patting of such heads as carried the best load of knowledge.

"Don't you think you have too much complacency in your school work?" inquired the Mother Superior as she listened to Sister Mary Paul's glowing description of her examinees' cleverness.

Her characteristic answer was:

"Dear Mother, is not humility truth, and does not truth make us free to rejoice at our personal success as well as to mourn at our failure? Teaching is so inspiring an occupation that I begin to suspect myself born to, rather than made for it; so, dear Mother, you see I have a holy complacency in examination results."

"Be sure that it is 'holy,'" warned the vigilant Mother Superioress.

Meanwhile, the ranks broken by the departure of the older nuns, were filled by efficient subjects, so that school work was accomplished successfully not only in Sister Mary Paul's department, but also in all the others. Music was taught in grades and its excellency was demonstrated at each recurring Commencement. Stringed playing received great attention and nothing escaped the musical vigilance of Sister Kostka Rosecrans, who directed the Academy and particularly the department of music. Consummate musician that she was, and we must not wonder how she was regarded by Sister Mary Paul, who again had complacency in knowing that such glorious talents were returned to God with the required gospel interest.

When persons of unusual talent were brought to her notice, she had often to commiserate the fact that they were not using at least some of their power for God, for she was wont to say, "These gifts are too great for worldly affairs." One evening, Karl Formes, the great basso, sang Benediction, and what a Benediction it was! It was to sound what a rich sunrise is to color. How he blended the salutatory grandeur of the "Salve Regina" into the moans of the "Gementes et flentes in hac lacrymarum valle"! Then the glorious Laudate at the end of Benediction made the congregation think that their feet were standing in the new Jerusalem and that some seraphic being was praising

God in a befitting manner. On this occasion, Sister Mary Paul expressed her feeling by saying, "Contentment filled my whole being, when I heard that wonderful voice put to the highest use, and God was given praises so artistically rendered."

The idea of dedicating to God and our Blessed Mother whatever was stamped with highest excellence was to her a matter of duty; for instance, one day, at the recreation hour, the picture of a beautiful novice was passed round among the senior students, one of whom remarked, "Miss —— is too pretty to bury herself in a convent. She should have remained in the world, where her beauty and talents would show to advantage."

"Is she too pretty for God?" asked Sister Mary Paul with unwonted asperity. Then with Samuel-like zeal she administered a rebuke sharp and stern to the offending young girl who would dare to defraud our "Sweet Lord" of the fairest from His flock.

Sister M. Paul was enemy to all affectation and insincerity among children. It mattered not how disagreeable the task of correcting might be, she applied herself to it with unceasing energy. These vices, apparently trifles light as air, seemed to her more deadly to the soul than poison is to the body. How kindly and vigorously did she help the victims of these inborn vices to cultivate the opposite virtues! How skilfully, too, did she settle differences! How she would lead children to examine the part that their likes and dislikes played in quarrels, and to turn their eyes upon the inner man always self-indulgent, so that becoming self-judges they might be able to pronounce their own condemnation and do penance!

Often she would direct a pupil's attention as to how men and things combine to become God's avengers upon breakers of the Ten Commandments. To the sinful, inanimate nature refuses its charm; the neighbor refuses the lovely side of his character; and sometimes sinners themselves commit suicide, because they loathe the sight of their own hideousness. She believed that salt duly boiled with food made it better than if mixed when cooked, so did she mix spiritual learning with secular, thereby seeking to produce a finer specimen of Christian; hence, when feasible, she led her pupils to the correlation of secular studies with religious. For instance, to a class pursuing geological periods, she would suggest a study of the Canticle of the Three Children in the Fiery Furnace, so that the class might note in what order inanimate nature was called upon to bless the Lord, how this order corresponded to the geological periods and completed the first climax of the sublime song. In like manner, the second climax invited animate nature to bless the Lord, and here was to be compared the chronological order of each creation with correlation in the secular text. This second climax reaches its highest when the sons of men are invited to bless the Lord. The third is a climax of sanctities, beginning with Israel, the highest types from the sons of men; next the sacerdotal order which connects these with the spirits and souls of the just; finally, reaching its last round when the sublime trio walking unhurt through the raging flames invite one another to bless the Lord forever. Nebuchodonosor, seeing the angel and hearing the heavenly quartette, utters his mandate of mercy. This twofold presentation takes us outside geological and secular realms and affords entertainment, spiritual, moral, and sublime.

The community had now grown to fifteen members and prosperity was increasing year by year.

It was at this time that a very bright little paper, called the "College Spy," was first written. Each issue was looked for with keen delight by the fun-loving students, and even the Reverend Pastor and the faculty did not think to jeopardize their dignity by their pleasurable anticipations. To the novices and rhetoric students, who evinced the smallest hope of the "poet's eye in a fine frenzy rolling," was allotted the writing of poems, one of which we subjoin, because being couched in allegorical form on the number and character of the fifteen foundation nuns and meeting the exactions of competition, it received from the Superioress the prize of "One Dollar!"

FOUNDATION STONES.

A Builder would rear a mansion
 To last forever I ween—
Selected from far away quarries,
 Some rocks, exactly fifteen.

With care and toil He brought them,
 O'er ocean and prairies vast,
Until in the land of the Sunset,
 He laid His stones at last.

To His men He gave directions
  To fashion these stones with care;
For they should be foundations
  Of a wondrous mansion, rare.

Nor chisel, nor hammer were spared,
  On these obdurate rocks fifteen,
Till they were fashioned and shaped,
  For that Architect's eye so keen.

"Now raise," said the Master-builder,
  "On these well-cut stones fifteen,
Such a firm and beauteous palace,
  As never before was seen."

"And further," continued the Builder,
  "My palace must stand alway;
Nor storm, nor rain can harm it,
  For its base is strong, I say."

Thus that edifice fair is rising:
  Shall it last forever, O say?
It will, if the hammer and chisel
  On the younger rocks will play.

And then the Master-builder
  With approving Face serene,
Will gaze on His castle splendid,
  That stands on His rocks fifteen.

The winner of the dollar being a novice, was told to use the money for anything she wished; hence, great was the consultation as to its most profitable investment. Far-seeing financiers suggested that the dollar be deposited with the Mother Superior at ten per cent.

interest: counselors with pious intent insisted that it should secure a Mass for the dead; while a third party unabashed by its epicurean propensities was loud in favor of a feast, and strange to say, this greedy contingent prevailed: but before the participants sat down to the banquet, they had incurred so large a debt that many prize poems were discussed to cover the liabilities. Such competitive and remunerative devices for improvement stole away much literary hardships and bestowed the joys of successful work. Sister Mary Paul lent herself with zest to these plans, and many a student owes a lucrative position to the department of humanities which, developing her latent talent, snatched her from among those who go down to their graves unsuspected monuments of hidden greatness.

Another later poem which received Sister Mary Paul's commendation was a parody on Poe's "Raven."

With admirable coolness, Sister M. Paul kept in check what threatened to be a severe panic among the young ladies caused by a stray member from the Native Sons' celebration of September 9th, one Admission Day.

The heat and fatigue of the day urged an unruly party to forget his discomfort in renewed acquaintance with Bacchus; then, in some way he stumbled to the door of the Convent. Mistaking the building for the hotel, he tugged violently to enter. His efforts awakened the children and a counterpart to Rosenthal's "Seminary Alarmed" followed. Sister Mary Paul, who, with the frightened boarders, occupied the dormitory, telephoned to the priest's house for help.

The stirring event is detailed as follows:

### A MIDNIGHT INCIDENT.

(With apologies to E. A. Poe.)

#### 1.

Once upon a midnight dreary,
While we slumbered tired and weary,
Over books hid 'neath our pillow,
Books quite full of courting lore—
Did we sleep, or were we napping,
When there came that sudden rapping,
As of some one roughly knocking—
Rapping at the Convent door.
"'Tis a thief," we said, "entreating
Entrance at our postern door—
Only this and nothing more!"

#### 2.

And the gingham—sad, uncertain rustle
Of each gingham curtain,
Filled us, thrilled us, with fantastic terror
Never felt before;
And each shivering, crying maiden,
Who from sorrow overladen,
Tried to keep her heart from beating,
So kept, off and on, repeating,
"'Tis a Native Son entreating
Entrance at our Convent door,—
Only this and nothing more!"

#### 3.

Presently our souls grew stronger;
Mother Paul could wait no longer,
And in telephonic language
Wired across two words or more—

"Come, O quick, good Father Cassin,
Your swift presence we implore—
For the fact is, we were napping,
And a burglar came a-tapping,
Rapping at our Convent door;
Girls are making noise galore—"
Quoth the priest, "Pray, say no more!"

4.

Right upon his elbow turning,
Angry thoughts within him burning,
Father heard again the message
More distressing than before;
Lightning speed was in his moving
And his pistols he looked o'er—
"I'll go too," said good Miss Cassin;
Pale she stood upon the floor,
But her brother scarcely heard her;
Fierce he shot through open door—
Then he shouted "Nevermore!"

5.

Deep into the darkness peering,
Poor Miss Cassin, praying, fearing,
Dreaming dreams, no mortal
Dared to dream before;
Ghastly grim she thought her brother
Flying through his chamber door.
"Not the least obeisance made he,
Not a minute stopped or stayed he,"
Said Miss Cassin in narrating
All the woes that night she bore—
These she told to Leonore.

#### 6.

Not a word her brother uttered,
Not a nerve within him fluttered;
Not the winds could beat him flying
Through that gloomy night of yore,
Running fast and running faster
Till he reached the Convent door,
Till he clutched the wretch a lying
With the lamp light gloating o'er—
And the dust of Day's carousal
Was upon the coat he wore:
Only this and nothing more.

#### 7.

Now the girls in great alarm
Fearing much some untold harm,
Muttered orisons that angels
Never heard from lips before.
Father Cassin found them praying
And this fact (the girls were saying)
Urged him quickly to the danger,
Made his wrath to quick outpour:
"Wretch," he said, "how cam'st thou hither?
Fly I say from Convent door."
"Reverence," quoth the wretch, "No more!"

#### 8.

Miss Mahoney near the casement,
Heard this parley at the basement,
And her prayers to saint or angel,
Little relevancy bore.
"Art thou Jew or French," said Father,
"That thou venturest near this door,
Or hath all the demons fired thee
From the dark Plutonian shore?"
Not a syllable expressed he,
Till he said, "You're right, asthore!"

9.

"Native Son," said Father Cassin,
"Your vague answer I deplore;
Tell me quick, hath Pluto fired thee,
Up against this Convent door?
For I cannot help agreeing
That no other living being,
Would so disrespect these precincts
As to hurl thee near this door;
And thy beard unshorn, unshaven—"
"Hold! your Reverence, I'm no craven—
Wine hath fired me—nothing more!"

10.

Father Cassin at the basement
Saw the maidens at the casement;
Stern contempt was in his aspect,
As their hands he did explore.
Water was in every basin
To let show'r on that Free Mason
Should he gain the Convent door—
Should he dare to take Lenore.
Angry, awful words suppressed he,
Fisting Native Son repressed he,
When he saw the basins pour.
"Xanthippe! ye Xanthippes!"
Was the priest's indignant roar—
Then led the man from Convent door.

# CHAPTER VIII.

Oppressed by failing health Rev. J. M. Conway was obliged to leave Santa Rosa; and, after severe mental and physical suffering, he finally passed to his reward. His remains were laid to rest among his first parishioners in London, Ohio.

His place was filled by the Reverend John M. Cassin, in whom Sister Mary Paul experienced God's unspeakable providence; for no priest could render more devoted attention to a community than he; and for nearly three decades of years, his untiring work has helped largely to make the Ursuline College what it is. In point of time, we are too near this man of God, to portray his manly and holy character: and, moreover, his deep humility would be wounded thereby; suffice it to say that a more devoted friend has seldom been given to a community than was given to the Ursulines of Santa Rosa in the person of Reverend John M. Cassin.

To Sister Mary Paul he was guide when too great zeal urged her to undertake that which could not be done well; he was her solace, when her work failing to bring the results she sought, threatened discouragement. However, her nature would not allow her to linger in the miasma of dejection, for she was par excellence an optimist, and she often quoted Wordsworth's optimistic quatrain which truly expresses her sentiments regarding neighborly intercourse:

> "I've heard of hearts unkind, kind deeds
> With coldness still returning;
> Alas! the gratitude of men
> Hath oftener left me mourning."

This gratitude from others came to Sister Mary Paul, because her own guileless soul rarely saw in them aught but good, and she had a way all her own that brought to the surface the virtues that she saw in others, and which the owners themselves did not dream that they possessed.

The vacation beginning June, 1889, found Mother Alphonse Costello quite ill. Her constitution, never robust, gave little hope of recovery. On June 16th, Trinity Sunday of that year, this saintly religious passed from life's stern conflict in the Church Militant to her well earned reward in the Church Triumphant, leaving her devoted Community to mourn their great loss.

For over thirty years, her little tombstone stood solitary in God's Acre, seeming to forbid companionship till at least some of the work she so ardently commenced was accomplished. It was the subject of this biography that broke the barrier of solitude and lay down to rest beside this valiant woman, this much revered Superioress, whose desire to see great things done for her beloved Santa Rosa was, perhaps, the reason why our dear Lord kept a phenomenal record of good health among the sisters whom she loved so well.

Perhaps also, nuns so strongly constituted withstood the ravages of time and the pressure of labor. This, together with a most salubrious climate and rooms flooded with beneficent sunshine, was a natural reason for soundness of body and mind. This blessed gift Sister Mary Paul enjoyed to its fullest, and truly had she need of it; for little leisure to nurse ailments is left to her who sees so much to be done in God's service with one's span of years so short at most.

Nothing more clearly illustrates the strength and beauty of our nature so much as does friendship, which brings forth our most charming manifestations, especially those of generosity and heroism. Surely we climb to heaven on the rounds of love, for the greater our charity towards our fellow creatures in general, the greater our love for the individuals whom we select from among them for the sacred intimacies of our inner selves. Pinnacled above all lesser friendships tower three groups of exemplars. The pagan group presents Damon and Pythias, noble Syracusans, standing on the scaffold vying with each other as to which shall secure the privilege of dying for the other. The strength of their love is shown in their extraordinary desire to suffer for each other, while their speech arouses the admiration of the witnessing multitude who rend the air with acclamations for pardon. The tyrant king, Dionysius, is rendered motionless by the sublimity of the spectacle and by the extraordinary dispute of the peerless friends. Below the stratum of his besottedness runs a tiny, unsuspected rivulet of manhood, which the power of the scene forces to the surface, opening a vent in these words:

"Live! live, ye incomparable pair! Ye have demonstrated to me that somewhere there exists a Supreme Being who has endowed you with one of His own attributes. Love such as this, can emanate only from Him!"

And Damon and Pythias, saved from the scaffold, descend amid the dithyrambic plaudits of the populace.

In the second group, the Jewish, we have for exemplars David and Jonathan, whose great friendship is glorified and immortalized by the Sacred Text. Count how many times it says: "Jonathan loved David as his own soul." Note the wondrous love in their dispute as to which shall secure the privilege of yielding Israel's throne to the other. Observe also how many times Jonathan risks his life for his cherished David.

But these friendships, exquisite though they were, dwindle into insignificance when we reach the highest pinnacle and contemplate the Divine Friend pillowing the head of his beloved John on His Sacred Heart. Here we have the very apotheosis of friendship, the guide for all mankind, who seek unspeakable calm for their weary head on the breast of a friend. O blessed passion of Love which abides with us after Faith and Hope, their great mission fulfilled, have passed away and only heaven remains! Thus the Divine Friend stands on the bridge of human love, a sacred model connecting past, present, and future with love chains, linking a St. Polycarp with a St. Lawrence, a

St. Francis de Sales with a St. Jane de Chantal, and numberless religious friends with friends.

Among the last, ranked Sister Mary Paul in her role of friend; and well did she copy her holy ancestors in respect to the claims of the most delicate of passions, which in her exuberant nature needed right direction and wholesome restraint.

Her friendship, removed from a chilling world, was transmitted into glowing loyalty which fulfilled its God-given mission; namely, happiness and security.

The trying months of noviceship and the small thorny paths leading up to profession were rendered less hard by the help of her "dear friend."

The elections consequent on the death of Mother Alphonsus were presided over by His Grace, Most Reverend P. W. Riordan, D. D., and resulted in the choice of Mother Agatha Superioress; Sister Mary Paul Assistant; and Sister Kostka Zelatrice.

These new officials were highly pleasing to our holy Assistant, not because she found herself second in authority, but because she praised God who had given her the favor of a Superior whom she not only loved but also esteemed for rare prudence in the difficult and arduous task of governing a religious community.

During Mother Alphonsus' administration, these qualities had been under the keen observation of the sisters, the ill-health of the former causing most of the work to be done by her Assistant now the Superioress-elect; hence the joy of Sister Mary Paul to have over her dear sisters one whom she believed would rule for their welfare.

What satisfaction Sister Mary Paul gave during her term of office, would be better understood, could the observer see the gayety and happiness of her spiritual children, whenever she went amongst them. Her conferences were full of unction, the outcome of her interior recollection and of her love for the charge entrusted to her by God. Her plan here was similar to that of her school-room work; "because," said she, "no matter what be our condition of life, the Commandments bind us, and upon them our spiritual structure must be raised."

She held in abhorrence anything that savored of comparisons either regarding the character of one's work or the hours of labor entailed. If such comparisons were remotely suggested, she was troubled that any one in God's house should be anything but radiantly happy when one, rather than another, had been selected to perform the heaviest labor in God's holy service. In her office she could not escape the inevitable task of reproving; but whenever this had to be done, she took care that the recipients of the reproof had, what she called, a good laugh before retiring. This little kindness of hers was so well known among pupils that they looked for some funny story on days upon which they deserved and received her censure. The funny story came just before night prayers, so that they generally knelt to pray calm and repentant, while the most thoughtful learned most useful lessons on cheerfulness under difficulties, especially difficulties resulting from one's own shortcomings.

The two virtues, simplicity and sincerity, she

deemed necessary to good breeding. "In the perfect lady, we recognize the perfect nun," she would say, and she insisted upon unobtrusive and delicate manners in contradistinction to those which are striking.

On one occasion, a child who had been over-mannerly, was marked low in the monthly honors for politeness. The child inquired the cause, whereupon Sister M. Paul answered, "My child, paradoxical though it appears, you received low standing because you were too polite." The child somewhat bewildered said naively, "I don't know what that big words means!"

"Go, dear, and hunt it up in your dictionary; then return and we will discuss the subject of good manners." Needless to say, the child was improved by the lesson, plus the knowledge of the "big word."

Now was knit the first sonnet of Sister M. Paul's religious life, the sextette thereof rounding out all the richness and beauty of which the octave had given promise. Her executive years closed this sextette and ushered in the fourth régime of the Santa Rosa Community. Truly did the sisters miss the saintly jurisdiction exerted over them, and it was equally painful to their Mother Assistant to resign her charge. She often declared that God had given her so much sweetness in her work, that she was loath to change it.

Time is the developer of theory and practice. Truly was it so in regard to the subject of our sketch. Often she would say with stimulating effect, "Whatever thy hand findeth to do, that do with all thy might." She herself obeyed to the letter this injunction and found therein the sweetness which she sought.

She was fully convinced of the beneficent results effected by little changes in one's daily routine; consequently she was ingenious in planning them. Later when Elmhurst Academy was purchased, she enjoyed going with the sisters to this beautiful home in Napa Valley making thereby pleasure of necessity; and since driving was preferred to other modes of travel, the sisters started early and journeyed leisurely; and lured by the stately ferns and wild flowers of the hills, they often gathered them, thus breaking the tedium of continuous driving.

A secluded spot, which from the steel blue color of the rocks, the sisters named "Blue Rocks" became their dining pavilion, canopied by blue sky. A pure stream gurgling over the rocks gave refreshing drink, while rich grass gave renewed vigor to the horses.

To give an idea of the scenic grandeur through which our picnickers pass in going from Santa Rosa to St. Helena, we ask the readers to ascend Rincon Hill, overlooking Rincon Valley, on a morning when Spring in full tide of adolescence is freeing vegetation from Winter's grasp and beautifying all with fresh shades of green; when She is gemming the turf with an inconceivable mixture of iridescence; when She is incensing the air from her thousand thuribles; when She is sending forth her warblers to utter Her gladness, till each sense is alive to Her glory. Above nearer to the clouds, She is manifesting her wildest moods with never a suggestion of gentleness; while hundreds of feet below in undulating grace lies the expanse of Sonoma Valley, wide and most fertile of vales. Here agricultural skill is doing its utmost to make it resemble a vast conservatory, and scientific experiments in Nature's secrets are carried on by Luther Burbank, California's wizard. From our viewpoint Rincon Hill, may be seen the modest spires and domes of Santa Rosa, while in the blue, hazy distance, a little more to the southwest, is the thriving town of Sebastopol.

Regaled by their meal at "Blue Rocks," our picnickers re-enter their carriage and descend the hill on the other side. Soon a flat stretch of road is reached which leads to the Petrified Forest. Entering this cemetery of trees, one is amazed to see hoary forest giants who, overpowered by a fearful deluge of lava in days of volcanic upheaval, were felled to the earth and buried deep in graves of tufa. Who shall say in what age they were entombed before commercial activities caused them to be exhumed! Sightseeing parties and geologists come to view these petrified monsters of metamorphosed vegetation. Sister Mary Paul, as eager as any, promises herself an object lesson here with her geology class.

The picnic day is far spent, when Mt. St. Helena and the foothills skirting Napa Valley are outlined against the sky. At this season of the year the summits and sides of mountain and hill vary from purple to pearly gray, then to a soft coral tint, and the green foliage, sending its sheen from below, makes a picture not to be forgotten.

"Great heights charm the eye," says Goethe, "but the steps leading thereto do not." Thus Mt. St. Helena, four-thousand five-hundred feet in height, is gloriously objective! This view, and especially the valley, is eulogized by M. S. Beers; and of those living in this mountain snuggery, just south of the "Switzerland of America," the following lines both truly and beautifully express their sentiments.

NAPA VALLEY.

I spied a beautiful valley,
  All nestled cosily down
In the lap of some grand old mountains,
  That were flecked in green and brown;
It was like a wondrous vision,
  Which comes in our purest hours,
Of the garden made in Eden,
  All filled with fruits and flowers.
And trees that were green forever;—
  With a river rippling through,
That waters the beautiful valley
  And its blossoms of every hue.
'Twas a land enriched with vintage,
  And flowing with honey and wine:
A valley, like that of Hermon,
  With its dews and gold sunshine.

John Ruskin when celebrating the thirteenth anniversary of his birthday was asked if he had spent a happy year. He replied, "It was the happiest of my life, because I think in common things; it is having too much to do which constitutes happiness." If this juvenile philosopher spoke truth, then must Sister Mary Paul have had a veritable elysium, as those could testify who witnessed the daily round of duties which gave little leisure to our sweet, unselfish laborer.

"Coming events cast their shadows before.". Elections were to be held on June 21, 1895, and as this date approached, the sisters began to anticipate the loss of their Mother's holy jurisdiction. All too quickly for their loving hearts came St. Aloysius' Feast whose evening found elections over, and Mother St. John in the chair of Superioress.

The ascetic spirit of the new Superioress urged her to concern herself more with the interior life of the community than with the exterior; consequently, bolts and screws of the inner life were fastened and tightened, and God was truly served under her strict direction. Though Sister Mary Paul had a constitutional regret to lay old ways aside, she was, nevertheless, as diligent in her loyalty to the new Superioress as she had been to the preceding. She was wont to say: "Dear, holy Mother St. J. will mold many a saint in our cherished community," and perhaps one of Sister Mary Paul's accidental joys in heaven is this knowledge. Soon after the election, Reverend John Rogers of Tomales requested the help of two sisters for his Sunday-school in Sebastopol, a growing city about seven miles from Santa Rosa. His zealous desire was promptly gratified by the services of Sisters U. and G. These rendered service of such merit that a great number of children are still yearly instructed and prepared for the Sacraments. The good work continues in unbroken interest, not only on the part of pastor and sisters but also on the part of parents and children. This extension of the teaching of Christian Doctrine in St. Sebastian's parish lifted from Sister M. Paul's shoulders the work she was wont to do among individuals residing at a distance.

Among the Sunday-school children enrolled have been many whose parents she instructed and "genuine little Romanists they are," said a non-Catholic lady, "which speaks volumes for the instruction of their fathers and mothers." The time afforded Sister Mary Paul by release from the Sebastopol Sunday-school work gave our zealous catechist more opportunity to devote herself to the spiritual needs of the young ladies of Santa Rosa through the Sodality of the Blessed Virgin; and the power for good exercised by these young women, can be estimated only when the veil is drawn and things are no longer seen in "a dark manner."

Miss Mary R., one of these Sodalists, thus describes her holy directress:

"What can I say of Sister Mary Paul's missionary work as Prefect of the Sodality? One thing I can affirm is that in all the years of our acquaintance, her aim was to keep the Sodality a purely spiritual body. Sometimes the girls would urge her to allow them to introduce innocent pleasures, but the answer was ever 'I think Father C. wishes us to make this a spiritual order only, and so it ought to be.' Then, too, her instructions to us were heart to heart talks, and I remember E—— saying on one occasion that she would rather listen to Mother M. Paul's instructions than to an eloquent sermon.

"But after our meeting proper was over, hand in hand, as many of us as could get near our beloved Mother, had our little walks over to the Convent from the church or hall. We then sat on the steps or walked around the paths, loath to leave; and in the pleasantry of the hour how the hearty laugh of Mother Paul could be heard! I remember her once asking a young girl if the gentleman in whom she was interested was a Catholic and if he attended church! 'Why, yes, Mother, he goes to church every Sunday evening.' How we all laughed! But Mother M. Paul, taking the remark seriously, instructed the young lady on the necessity of going to church a little earlier in the day. She understood us, brought out the best that was in us, and interested herself in our home life and future. Then, too, how much she did for those not of the Sodality! I have in mind a boy who attended to his religious duties and said the Litany of Loretto every day, because he had promised Sister M. Paul to do so. I could quote many similar examples, but let one suffice. Oh! bright, happy moments spent in her holy company! Surely we were privileged for her leadership!"

The following letters though written some years later, will exemplify her holy encouragement to a young sodalist aspiring to the religious life:

"Ursuline Academy, St. Helena, Sept. 14, 1911.
"My dear M———

"Yesterday your sweet letter was received. I am delighted to see you still reaching for the Great Ideal; soon it will be within your grasp, the Feast of

St. Ursula would be an auspicious day for you to take the first step. If you have not sent in your application to Mother Superior, I would advise you to do so at once; however, you must consult Rev. Father C. and be guided by his decision as to the time of leaving home. Dear Father C. baptized you. I prepared you for First Communion from which time you have been faithful to God's whisperings. How delighted Father C. will be to receive from his dear spiritual child M. the vows of Poverty, Chastity, Obedience, and Charity or Institute. You will keep the lamp of Chastity always burning in your hand, you will feed it with the oil of Charity, and replenish it with the perfume of Humility. Then when death comes, you will confidently hail the summons to arise and go forth to meet the Bridegroom to remain forever in His fond embrace. Please tell your mamma and papa that Sister Mary Paul says, 'the privilege of leaving all to find all, is on Margaret's side.' Religion does not crush the natural affection; it purifies and ennobles filial instincts, makes us wish our loved ones well and inspires ardent prayer, that they may reach the Highest Goal, God Himself, when the days of severe probation in a world of temptation and strife, are done forever."

To the same.

"My dear M———:

"I am delighted to read from your kind letter your sweet determination of giving yourself to Almighty God under the banner of our own dear Mother St. Angela. You, dear M——— will be the gainer for time and eternity. Do not delay when you hear the voice of God speaking to you through your revered spiritual Father. Enter just when he decides.

"The permission which you will be obliged to get from the Most Reverend Archbishop need not cost you any anxiety, and Rev. Father C. will give you a letter of introduction before you go to see His Grace. Present yourself as soon as possible. Answer simply any question the Archbishop may ask you. Then you will return to Santa Rosa with the approval of His Grace on your holy determination of being admitted into the Convent of the Ursulines, there to live under the same roof with our dear, sweet Lord till you hear the Heavenly Bridegroom's call to your Eternal Home: 'Come, child of My Heart, thou art at rest!' Here are a few lines dedicatory of the new life you are about to enter upon here below:

> "Jesus hidden on the altar,
>   More than all the world to me,
> Had I all things without Jesus,
>   Earth, a dreary waste would be."

"As soon as you return from San Francisco, write me how you enjoyed your visit to the Most Reverend Archbishop. Say one Hail Mary to our Lady of Good Counsel daily in these days of immediate preparation for entering the convent. If you do this, you need fear nothing, for our dear Mother Mary in answer to your prayer will be your guide."

Another letter to the same after the Ceremony of Reception:

"My dear Sister G――――, Congratulations!

"Your sweet letter came, making my heart rejoice to learn that at last you are safe in God's House. What a privilege! And to think that you are called by the name of one of Jesus' most loving Spouses! You know it is said of our dear Lord that to repose in the heart of Gertrude was His chief delight. And why?—Because her heart was so pure, so generous, and so much like to His own Sacred Human Heart. Think of this, when you go to Holy Communion. I am glad you are studying Latin with dear Sister P――――, also that you are continuing your music. Do all these things for the pure love of God so that you may be more useful among the children. Eat well, sleep well, and laugh well. I think you will become a favorite child of your saintly Mistress of Novices. Try to imitate her. Ask our Lord daily to make you love the spirit of your holy vocation. Be humble. Be kind. Do not try to appear learned. Be your own true self, and you will lead many souls to God. Courage! O, what a consolation to go to confession! You must tell dear Reverend Father C―――― anything that might trouble you. Speak only of self, and keep that down as much as you can."

A New Year's letter:

"Dear Sister G———:

"A very happy New Year! I am delighted to hear you are well, but just think, dear, 'all the beauty of the King's daughter is within.'

"Some day your family will see their dear M——— seated on the triumphal car of Jesus under the banner of St. Angela among all the dear Ursulines of Santa Rosa, driving through the New Jerusalem and singing the new canticle, which only virgins will sing—and what beatitude for all Eternity! Courage! Be good. Be obedient. Life is a vapor that appears for a short time, then vanishes: but, like the same vapor, should tend skyward. Send your aspirations in this direction and fear not. Keep self in the background, and Jesus will place you in the foreground with His favored ones."

The following letter to the same written on the eve of Sister Mary Paul's death is remarkable:

"November 13, 1912.

"My dear Sister G———:

"Your first feast in the Convent! Congratulations! How far have you climbed on the 'Golden Ladder'? I hope you are quite high on it by this time. Remember that when you reach the top, you will find our dear Lord waiting to greet His dear faithful spouse, and to crown her with an everlasting diadem of glory in Heaven. Courage! A few short years away from a wicked world, then an everlasting reward!

"May dear St. Gertrude obtain for you and yours a practical Faith accompanied by good works. What a day of rejoicing when you and all your dear ones will be safe in Heaven! Courage, I repeat. Life is short. 'A day quickly passed.'

"Be charitable. Be prayerful. Jesus will be with you. 'Forget thy people and thy father's house, and the King will greatly desire thy beauty.' Your people will be cared for by Him, who is never outdone in generosity. Fond love to all the family. My love to your saintly Mistress of Novices, and to all the novices. Please tell dear Sister B—— 'that I will answer her note as soon as I find time. The Ursuline 'rush' is now in Elmhurst on account of the big parish school."

After Mother St. J—— had, with holiness and profit served her term of office, Mother A—— was reinstalled as Superioress. Again Sister Mary Paul felt the goodness of God in accordance with her desire as to the issue of elections. "I feel as if I were treading on thin air," she said, when she returned from the congratulatory exercises incident on the re-inauguration of her former Superioress. Many times on this auspicious day did she draw near to the Holy of Holies to pour forth her gratitude for the morning's graces; and many times did she comment on the same with companions.

The following day was one of general recreation, which relieved both the strain of the late retreat and the anxiety consequent on elections. Under the umbrageous oaks and spreading willows in the open, flower-scented air and to the singing and chirping of the inhabitants of the trees, was served a genuine picnic dinner. Reverend J. M. C., the loved and honored guest, beguiled the time with inimitable stories and reminiscences from his life of crowded and felicitous experiences.

Dinner over, the diligent Marthas of the festivity sit down to table amidst prolonged applause, which gives time for a group of Marys to begirth themselves with aprons and other appurtenances for the equal success of the second contingency. Their further duty is to leave all things ready for an out-door supper, since the whole day must be enjoyed in the open.

In the afternoon are exhibited feats of skill in tennis; or that comforting feminine instrument, the needle, is seized by the more practical, and presto! they lash out on linen or silk, spreading artistic patterns over the goods soon to be converted into the sacred use of the Altar as vestments, Tabernacle curtains, and the like.

Ah! me! fair days of monastic peace, of innocence and culture, why are you not better known, why are there so few to sit at Jesus' Feet, like our holy Sister Mary Paul, to drink deeply the inebriating draughts of His Love, saying, "Lord, it is good for us to be here"? But the shades of night come on apace and the Office bell calls to prayer. An onlooker of the day's proceedings would say, "You lucky ones are having your hundredfold here." But the promise of Eternal life is the hundredfold at infinite interest!

Life is so checkered with joy and sorrow, that the more reflective learn how to prepare for the one, while experiencing the other; and in these experiences of joy and sorrow Sister Mary Paul had, as we have seen, no small share. The joyful part of her existence was soon suspended, and in spirit we now find her walking with the Morrissey family on the Via Crucis; for her beloved mother is about to leave her loved ones for heaven.

But not as the Cyrenean took the Cross of Christ did the Morrisseys take theirs. Lovingly and ungrudgingly they bore it so that their mother's passing was as peaceful as her life had been.

Pillowed on the strong arm of one of her faithful sons, she lay, her voice answering the prayers for her own entrance to Eternity; her lips frequently kissing the crucifix; her children with the exception of the one consecrated to the service of God, present.

In the family of Patrick and Sarah Morrissey, the proverbial black sheep was conspicuous by absence; for with the vigilance of the earthly angel guardian that Mrs. Morrissey was, had she not seen to it that the whiteness of her children's souls should not be sullied? And now as her eyes dwelt lovingly upon each face, she saw that fine manhood and womanhood had left an imprint to console her dying moments. More potent than words were the looks that said: "Behold we are and shall be with God's help followers of you, O sweet mother, and we shall meet you again when the rains shall cease and the shadows vanish." As the clock struck the hour of two in the early morning, the soul of this devoted mother departed this life to hear the comforting invitation, "Come! Thou blessed of my Father."

The following notice of Mrs. Morrissey's death gives some idea of the esteem in which she was held by the parishioners of St. Mary's Church:

"At St. Mary's Church this morning (September 29, 1900), the funeral of Mrs. S. Morrissey was held, and there were many sympathizing friends present at the final obsequies. A solemn requiem Mass was sung over the remains by Reverend Lewis Bellew, C. P., celebrant; Reverend Theodore Noonan, C. P., deacon; and Reverend Edmund P. Hill, C. P., subdeacon.

"Reverend Father Lewis, a friend of the departed woman, delivered the funeral sermon. After depicting the beautiful life of the deceased, and how happy her closing moments were in being fortified in soul by the Church's sacraments, he sympathized with the bereft ones in the loss of the mother who had been ever watchful and careful of their ways, and exultant in their success; and whose memory in turn should ever be embalmed in grateful hearts. The loss of a mother is always a great bereavement, for it hushes the heart which to childhood was a refuge; the parental heart, which was always the source of quickest sympathy and the sharer of joys and sorrow. Upon the hearts of those bereft, ill winds blow over a wide wilderness of desolation, and desert sands drive across the place which once bloomed like a garden of God.

"For many years Mrs. Morrissey was a member of St. Mary's Church. She was one blessed with the inestimable gift of Faith, and she gloried in the thought that she had given to the Church from among her children one, who, at death's hour, was praying for the aged one about to give up life's struggle.

"After the last prayers in the Church, the remains were interred in St. Mary's cemetery, where the final absolution was given by Reverend Aloysius Blakely, C. P., an old-time friend of the departed woman.

"The floral offerings were many and beautiful, including a large broken column, emblematic of the loss of a loved one, pillows, wreaths, and cut flowers. Floral designs were given by city officials, school children and by teachers of School No. 3. The body was laid to rest in a vault where it will find surcease forever from labor, sorrow, and trouble.

"At the funeral were many school teachers and pupils of the different schools, as well as a delegation of city officials, including the Common Council. The departments of the city government closed their offices during the morning out of respect to City Engineer Morrissey, son of the deceased."

Sister Mary Paul's letter given below expresses her feelings on her mother's death, which being caused by pneumonia, was somewhat sudden.

"J. M. J. U. A.
"Ursuline Convent, Sept. 27, 1900.
"My cherished brothers and sisters:
"A few hours ago, I received the telegram requesting me to pray for our dear mother, who is

dying. Though it is now twenty-one years since I bade her good-by, I have not neglected to pray for her, that God would give to her a peaceful death; and now that He is about to send His angel to take her pure soul to join that of our dear father, let us thank God for His mercy. I know as well as you, beloved people, that it is hard to part with one so dear as our saintly mother: but she is only going home before us, to pray for us and to await gladly our coming, one by one, till the Morrissey family of Sheridan Center will be again united never to be separated.

"I am sure that all the dear Passionists who knew her will say Holy Mass for her. Do not weep too much, dear brothers and sisters, as that would not be pleasing to our dear mother.

"I know you will all recall the example of a true Christian that she gave us, when dear father was suddenly snatched from us. I can never forget it; a house full of young children around her, when she heard the cruel news of his sudden death!—immediately, with silent grief, so Godlike, she entered her bedroom and on bended knees she offered to God the heavy blow which had struck her. O what an example of pure and holy faith was this! let us follow this example of our death mother; let us keep God's Commandments as perfectly as we can in this land of exile, and then we shall soon—O! very soon —hear the same summons to join our dear parents. I have offered many prayers and actions that our saintly mother would not only die a peaceful death but also one without pain in the arms of Jesus, Mary and Joseph, and my prayer is about to be heard.

"Now my beloved brothers and sisters, be patient and resigned. God takes from you the sensible presence of our fond and loving mother but for what?—O, to take her home and to crown her with Immortality! Please to write me all the particulars of her holy death. I will be with you in spirit at the church, at the grave, and at the lonesome home, when you return from the last sad rites. Again asking you all to be brave and generous through this ordeal, I will close. I know that God will give you courage and strength to bear it as our darling mother would have wished.

"I will ask dear Reverend Father C .... to say holy Mass for her on next Saturday. Tomorrow he has a funeral Mass. Our Community will go to Holy Communion for our mother, and, of course, I shall as long as I live be indebted to her for her care of us, and endeavor to pay my indebtedness by continued prayer.

"With love to all and gratitude to Almighty God for His mercy and tenderness to the Morrissey family . . . . ."

---

Six years later, on April 18th, 1906, the dread temblor undid in twenty seconds, the work that millions of men had accomplished in a century. Not only did the fair Metropolis of the Golden West lie prostrate under his tortuous route, but also the suburban towns and cities. Among the latter was the neat little City of Roses, where the pitiless devastation of fire worked with such violence as to level the city nearly to the ground. Heaps of timber, pipes, and household materials remained, while the ghastly horror of what might be revealed when men could gather strength to remove the debris, was the worst anticipation of all. In this catastrophe, the impress of the Divine Face was nowhere to be seen; but relentless demons, conspiring with the unreasoning agents of nature, apparently ruled the hour, so that when people recovered speech, it was used to comment on God's attitude towards the world, as He was then manifesting Himself to this afflicted portion.

"If there be a God," said the skeptical, "and He allows this suffering, we want none of Him." Others maintained that California had gone far from God's Commandments, and, like another Sodom, it was doomed to destruction. Saintly souls, too, had something to say. Hope and cheer were the burden of their speech, and among the optimistic was Sister Mary Paul, who said, "The Face of God is only momentarily hidden behind the smoke and flame." But while she believed this, and knew that His Almighty power was restraining Nature's forces with the nicety of adjustment belonging to His omniscience, she looked with awe on the murky masses of smoke heaving skyward, turning day into night. In comparison:

"Surely, the things that we do,
Are the sports of a child to the infinite View."

Scientists, busy with their seismographs and other aids to man's puny knowledge (never more puny than when struggling in so fearful a crisis) were gathering what information they could on the temblor's fearful activities.

That God rarely interferes with physical laws was the comment of some. Others, whose minds soared never outside the boundaries of their laboratories, insisted that the earthquake was a mere natural phenomenon which might be repeated any time before the sun went down on April 18th. But as the hours of dismal forebodings dragged on and the dread Visitor did not conform to the conjectures of Job's comforters, people began to return to a sense of the work before them. The temblor had taken care to twist water-pipes into a net-work of inutility; and fire had already spent its force; therefore, all must be up and doing.—Were not the birds singing wild Te Deums with the jubilation that imperiled nature feels when safety succeeds? Were not cool zephyrs playing among trees and flowers as if in mockery of people's anguish? Was not sunshine flooding the ruins till all nature's manifestations seemed on a mission of mockery? The very "Regina Coeli Laetare" in the Divine Office of the season took on a strange mocking ring to hearts attuned to the "Dies Irae" so that human beings alone seemed excluded from the thanksgiving of God's creatures.

In these sad hours, Sister Mary Paul's familiar figure might be seen seeking our Lady's shrine or consoling some poor stricken one who sought the holy grounds to pour the day's sorrow into her sympathetic ear. The shrine was a favorite resort in those days as the chapel was considered unsafe.

The Sunday following, Reverend Father C . . . celebrated Holy Mass on the Convent grounds, where an unwonted congregation had assembled to worship and to be consoled by their Pastor's touching words in exposition of the inspired Word of God, so generously doled to the hearers, who now especially hung on his utterances for light and strength of soul. If the chief mission of speech is to unite man with man by communication of ideas, to soothe and comfort in the season of distress like this, how good is its mission! More effective and ennobling does it become, when uttered amidst the witcheries of artistic singing to the accompaniment of stringed instruments. This thought actuated the Sisters, who, for so memorable a Mass, put forth their talents, and what with Sister C . . . at the harp and Sister E . . . at the harmonium, and the splendid voices of Sisters A . . . and M . . ., the people received the benefit of the mission of the human voice, and were comforted and uplifted.

Following the singing in its: "Deep night hath come down on us, Mother," and the reiterated "We look for Thy shining, Sweet Star of the Sea," fresh confidence buoyed up the courage of the listeners and revived trust in the Almighty Fatherhood of God whose message in this earthquake visitation seemed to

View looking South

The Shrine

read: "I have punished you here that I may spare you Hereafter"—a memorable Sunday this, to be writ in the annals of the California Ursulines!

When Sister Mary Paul realized that April 18th was the feast of Blessed Mary of the Incarnation, America's first Ursuline, there was no doubt in her mind, but that the personal safety of the sisters and the miraculous preservation of the buildings were due to the intercession of her spiritual ancestor. O happy we, whose religious ancestors have left us the great legacy of their heroic lives! more happy we, when we use that legacy in accordance with the will of the testatrix; most happy we, when, having put that legacy out at the highest rate of interest, we receive our reward and in turn transmit the same augmented to our descendants.

"Surely," said Sister Mary Paul, "it was our Blessed Mother Mary of the Incarnation who inspired the 'Elks' to provide with incredible speed bread enough to keep Santa Rosa from serious hunger for several days." Such generosity from all outside the convent, coupled with extraordinary unselfishness on the part of those within, caused our holy sister to say, "It's like living amongst the early Christians."

This letter written on the day of the earthquake speaks for itself:

"Santa Rosa, Cal., April 18, 1906.
"To my dear brothers and sisters:

"Thank God we are saved from the 'jaws of the earthquake.' At about 5:30 A. M. we were visited by a terrible shock. Nearly all Santa Rosa is destroyed, Post Office, Court House, etc. We do not know yet how many persons have been killed. The Convent and the priest's house with the inmates of both houses are safe with no one even hurt. The church is slightly damaged. Following the earthquake, owing to the falling in of roofs and the danger of live wires, fire with its devastating consequences, began to rage. This indeed was our terror.

"The children all assembled in the chapel and said the Rosary at 10 A. M., but they recited the Litany of the Saints outside as fear for safety in the chapel was aroused.

"How wonderful are the ways of God! The labor and skill of man's greatest works can in a moment become dust. Be good, dear people, only goodness and nobility of life live Beyond! Santa Rosa has often experienced a light shaking of the earth, but this morning made us realize how terrible is an earthquake. Would you please have a Mass said in thanksgiving for the preservation of our Sisters and pupils? Also say the Rosary that God may be better known and loved in California. Dear, patient Mother Superior is somewhat overcome with the dreadful shock. Thank God for His Mercy to us all! Thank God! is all I can say."

"April 23, 1906.
"My dear Brother J . . . :

"Your telegram just received. O! dear brother, thank God we are all safe. Our dear little City of Roses is sadly ruined, and poor old San Francisco nearly destroyed. The Convent stands—a monument of God's mercy to us. On Sunday last Reverend Father C . . . said both Masses on our Convent grounds, where the beautiful sky was the dome of the lovely temporized Altar. The nuns and children sang at the first Mass and the nuns alone at the second. For the time being, all felt that they were in a new and supernatural place, separated from the harrowing scenes but a few blocks away, for besides the havoc, some people were killed and some burned in the catastrophe. I sent to M . . . a paper which will tell you of the destruction in San Francisco. Some feel that the earthquake is a visitation from Almighty God for the pursuit of wealth and pleasure, which has taken possession of our people, while God's Law is forgotten. However, His justice is tempered by His Mercy, and many are saved. There is a big-heartedness in the men of California, not found perhaps in any other state, but its people need to worship God and thus make California a most favored State—even though earthquakes do come sometimes. It is said that the region west of the Sierras is an upheaval and we may have volcanic activity from time to time.

"We are praying hard during the continuance of this disaster, that God's anger may be appeased, and that peace, Christian hope, and a new life may be infused into all. Soon our fair City, with its big sister San Francisco, will rise a better, a stronger, and a more beautiful God-like one than before."

One of the victims of the temblor writes thus

of Sister Mary Paul: "I shall never forget her, nor how all wanted her near them. Her presence seemed to bring us peace; the reassuring pressure of her soft little hand and her kind, holy words were like balm to our stricken hearts. Her happiness knew no bounds when she spoke to those of us who, unscathed by the disaster, had come to see how the nuns fared. How fervently she took us before the Blessed Sacrament and remained with us while we poured out our thanksgiving, and how fervently also did she make the sign of the Cross on our foreheads! Like our dear Lord Himself, she bade us fear not. During this dreadful time of restless repose, how often we would see her in our dreams ministering to the injured! The angel of the earthquake we thought her and truly we were not mistaken, for Sister Mary Paul was more angel than human."

## CHAPTER IX.

On May 4th, 1906, feast of St. Monica and the anniversary of the landing of Blessed Mary of the Incarnation on the shores of that historic citadel, Quebec, Sister Mary Paul celebrated the Silver Jubilee of her holy Profession; but for obvious reasons a spiritual celebration was all that could take place. However, her sisters united with her in gratitude for the signal preservation from earthquake and fire and for their ability to resume the work of St. Angela.

It was joy enough to see, that by degrees affairs were assuming normal conditions and that faces of friends were less fear-stricken. Past despair was giving way to hope. The cheer which Sister Mary Paul had hitherto forced was becoming genuine; and as people were growing more natural, they were able to see the humor of some happenings, so that faint smiles were broadening into healthy laughter. Sister Mary Paul dwelt on the kindness of God's mercy which gives the laugh as well as the tear, and Reverend Father C . . .'s reiterated: "A shock like this may not occur again for a century," gave solidity to the platform of cheerfulness upon which she stood and upon which she desired her friends to stand.

The family of Sister Mary Paul had long been looking forward to her Jubilee as a suitable time to make a request; namely, that they most earnestly desired to see their sister, and since they were so many in the family it became a question whether Mohammed should go to the mountain or the mountain to Mohammed. The former alternative having prevailed, they earnestly requested a visit from Sister Mary Paul. However much her nature acquiesced, she, nevertheless, kept herself in a state of indifference and merely answered that whatever was the will of God and of her Superiors, that she would accomplish. It was not until June, 1908, that God's will was made manifest by the permission being granted; and following the short delay of immediate preparation for the trip, Sister Mary Paul and her invited companion, Mother A . . ., found themselves speeding eastward.

From a letter written to her brother before the trip, we extract the following:

"Sometimes I forget your kind offer, but when it comes to my mind, it fills my soul with sweet consolations. I will be so happy to see you all, especially your darling babies. I am happy to take dear Mother A . . . with me, who has not only been my Superioress for nearly twenty-five years off and on, but also the tenderest of mothers, so that I shall be pleased to share with her that trip home, through you, dear brother. You will all love her for her almost divine simplicity, and greatness of character."

The Sunday which occurred within the days of travel, dawned as the Sisters reached Glenwood Springs; and as connection was not immediate, our travellers had time to hear holy Mass. Sister Mary

Paul with her wonted devotion became the self-constituted server. Mass over, the gracious celebrant, Reverend Father O'Dwyer, invited his guests to breakfast.

Toward evening, the travellers reached the convent of the Sisters of Mercy at Manitou. Mother Ignatius, the Superioress, received her guests with sisterly cordiality and lodged them in a room of unusual elegance, which troubled our poverty-loving Sister Mary Paul. But on hearing that it was a source of revenue to the Convent, because patients desiring such a suite of rooms paid well for their use, she hesitated no longer.

The following morning, Mother I . . . inquired if her guests had rested well. Sister Mary Paul replied: "Mother, when I overcame my astonishment at the bed canopied in purple velvet and the superb furnishings of the room, I slept quite well."

"No marvel that you were astonished," said the amused hostess, "when I tell you that by some historic luck, we are now the possessors of the couch of Josephine Bonaparte."

"Is it not a mystery how a woman of Josephine's character could not turn the ambition of her husband into other channels than those of blood?" said Sister Mary Paul.

"Perhaps," Mother A . . . rejoined (playing on the word Bonaparte), "his name had something to do with making him what he was. He parted, disjointed, rended, and buried more human bones than his prototype Alexander the Great."

"The French signification of the name would be more complimentary to the great little man," said Mother I . . ., but Sister Mary Paul agreed with Lowell:

> "He alone is base
> Whose love of right is for himself
> And not for all the race."

The arrival of the driver to take the travellers to the station put an end to comment, and in a few minutes the Sisters were en route to the top of Pike's Peak. The brave little engine pulling over trusty cogs and the quasi-conductor discoursing on the scenic interest of the ascent: they meanwhile were mounting past the timber line, past cavernous holes charred and vast, past pools black and fathomless; past dizzy precipices, past uncanny lakes swinging above the world. Along the trail was writ by mysterious pens appalling texts from Scripture and other sources, until Dante's Inferno seemed scarcely a circumstance to the awesome dread of God's vengeance conjured up by scene and text.

Finally the summit was reached, and before Sister Mary Paul looked out over the world stretched below her, regardless of the gale that threatened to take away her breath and the crowd of heterogeneous religionists that stood around, she fell on her knees and recited a "Laudate," devoutly emphasizing the "montes et colles" and the "spiritus procellarum."

The vast horizon removing all obstructions, there

could be seen at seemingly short distances Colorado Springs, Denver, Cripple Creek, Pueblo, Canon City, and the snow-clad Rockies hundreds of miles away. "No wonder that man's greatest supernatural events took place on mountains," said Sister Mary Paul to her companion. "From Ararat to Sinai, from Sinai to Nebo, from Nebo to Olivet, from Olivet to Calvary—what a trail of holy travel! and what transcendent things are the mountains themselves! Prayer seems the fittest expression of my feelings here," she continued.

Below lay the sin-tossed world; above reigned infinite peace glorified by the risings and settings of suns.

The Cave of the Winds next claimed the Sisters' attention. Its heavy darkness, its cavernous chambers and stalagmite statuary revealed by flashlights, the colossal figures of Lot's wife and other celebrities are so described by geographers that little is left to add, except that the Cave of the Winds and this Garden of the Gods surpass, to Sister Mary Paul's mind, the experience of Telemaque in Calypso's abode or the enchanted palaces of fairy lore.

As the time of travel was limited, the Sisters reluctantly bade adieu to Colorado, and in a few days they found themselves in Dunkirk, New York, in the midst of friends whose hunger for the sight of their loved one was at last satisfied.

Among her very own, Sister Mary Paul had the bliss of spending a few weeks, and who shall describe the happiness that she brought them, or the comfort they brought her in their blameless lives! She confided to Mother A . . . that she could sing, "Dismiss me, O Lord, for my eyes have seen my people serving and loving Thee beyond all else!" Scenes dear to her childhood, the Church in which she offered her young life, the beloved Passionist Fathers, the spots where slept the remains of her worthy parents—all were lovingly visited. Verily her people had found a season of happiness wherein they would fain live and ward off the inevitable parting, which came, however: and, be it said that "the veil which hides the future is woven by angel hands," for it mercifully shut out in this parting the knowledge that this was to be their last meeting on earth, notwithstanding each hopeful ruse which relatives press into service to mitigate the agony of farewells. But she, leaving behind her the sunshine, turned into the dark night of "nevermore" where hands do not clasp, nor lips meet; neither are words of love, though conjectured, spoken. But God's Holy Will was the lever by which Sister Mary Paul's soul was uplifted. The train pulled out from Dunkirk and headed for the great Metropolis.

In St. Angela's Ursuline College, New Rochelle, New York, she met some old friends and made new ones. Her enthusiasm knew no bounds, when she saw the splendid achievements of her Sisters both here and in Bedford Park at Harlem, N. Y. Her devotion was stirred by the stately manner in which the Divine Office was recited to organ accompaniment. How restful the holy atmosphere of the place! How queenly Mother Irene, the Superioress! Christian progress and culture permeate New Rochelle, the "Catholic Vassar" as St. Angela's College is called by those who compliment it on its secular attainments. "Was not our visit here a dream of religious neighborliness?" said Sister Mary Paul, as later, she sat on the deck of the "Harvard," on its maiden trip to Boston, which City was in the itinerary of our travelers.

Reverend Father T . . ., C. S. P., a former pupil of Sister Mary Paul, met her, and needless to say, this reverend friend outdid himself in showing favors to his beloved teacher. The Governor of Rhode Island, Hon. James Higgins, whose family were most dear to the Sisters, constrained them to spend a brief time in Pawtucket.

The Canadian Pacific route, which Sister Mary Paul preferred for her home journey, gave opportunity to visit Cliff Haven and the Ursulines of Quebec en route. Her impressions of these places may be better understood from her letters. She writes:

"My dear ones:

"How have you been since Mother Superior and I saw you looking so disconsolate? How cruel the acceleration, the roar, and the rush of the train as it hurled miles between you and me! Now I am sailing on Lake Champlain toward Ticonderoga. Sr. M. M. of Burlington, a guest of the Gray Nuns, is with us. A party of doctors is also here; for a terrific storm is so scaring the doctors' wives, that the ladies think themselves safe near us. This makes me very humble at my unworthiness of their confidence. These doctors know Governor Higgins and pronounce him to be a man that never utters falsehood, never drinks, never cheats, and one of the whitest-souled men in the State. You can imagine how pleased we were to hear this.

"We are taking this historic trip through the kindness of Rev. J. Mullany and his charming sisters. Our meeting them is the nearest we shall ever get to their gifted brother. What pleasure we had in discussing his works! Dear Brother Azarias! How proud they are of his vocation to the Christian schools! Mother A . . . was greatly interested in this meeting, and also in that of Reverend John Talbot Smith, and generous Father Thomas McMillan, C. S. P. We think their Cliff Haven is the acme of pleasurable education."

The arrival of Sister Mary Paul in Quebec in July 1908, followed close upon the tri-centenary celebration of the City's foundation in 1608. The tawdry of dead garlands, the skeletons of things that were, and the paper-bestrewn streets suggested Moore's "Banquet Hall Deserted"; but from the appearance of wrecked decorations, the fête must have been of splendid spectacular interest. One feature of the celebration was the Sisters' acceptance of the invitation to participate in the civic function; accordingly the Ursulines went outside their boundary and rounded out this truly historical pageant. The Ursuline Monastery, be it known, is in point of time, one of Quebec's foundation stones. Its beginnings were in 1639.

After the formula of securing the Archbishop's permission, our travellers were admitted within the cloister of the Convent and were received by the daughters of Blessed Mother Mary of the Incarnation, America's foundress of the Ursuline Order. Their reception had in it love, simplicity, and enthusiasm, which found in Sister Mary Paul a kindred spirit. When she was greatly impressed she was eager to share her feelings with others, for "Happiness was born a twin," and therefore, she took the first opportunity to send the following letter to Santa Rosa:

"My dear sweet Sisters:

"Mother A . . . and I are so bubbling over with Order-pride, that I send you these few lines to tell you how we are impressed with the Ursulines of Quebec.

"Mother says our feet are not exactly standing in the New Jerusalem: but in the courts paved and planned by Blessed Mary of the Incarnation. She is not dead, for her spirit is still training and drawing to our Lord the nuns and children of Quebec. The Sisters have preserved as much as possible the buildings which she reared. In these the very holes made by the contending cannon of the French and English are so covered that by opening a slide one can see the original walls bulleted by cannon.

"We arrived at an opportune time, because a few days previous the Prince of Wales and his staff had been entertained here, and the things of historic interest which had been shown him had not been replaced; hence, we had the satisfaction of seeing the exhibit. The skull of Montcalm with a few teeth in the upper jaw was the most interesting. When his Royal Highness saw the skull, he asked to be conducted to the tomb of the French hero. "Why did they not bury the skull with the rest of his body?" inquired the Prince. Mother Superior replied that monastic folk have ever safeguarded not only history proper but also concrete things appertaining thereto.

"We prayed in the little chapel in which Mass had been said by the Jesuit missionary Father Jogues and by other victims of Indian revenge. The chapel and altar are scarcely disturbed from the time these holy martyrs used them. At one side of this altar and covered with a rich crimson pall is a casket containing the bones of Mother Mary of the Incarnation, Mother St. Joseph, and Madame de la Peltrie. The humble dwelling of the last named with its quaint windows and gables, still stands. The past is so merged into the present, that one is puzzled as to the nearness of the one and the apparent remoteness of the other. We took dinner with the community in the great refectory, and after we had partaken of the soup, the Superioress gave a signal, whereupon was rendered a burst of song in harmonious parts: the decorum of the sisters and the burden of the song with its 'Ecce quam bonum' effect, were soul-stirring and devotional in the extreme. On the conclusion of this unique number, we were loath to return to the material things of life—to eat and make merry. But the holy Superioress bade us take recreation, an unusual privilege in this refectory, where during meals 'the mouth not only receives its nourishment, but the ear, by spiritual reading, is also filled with the word of God.'

"Mother St. Croix, a near relative of Oliver Wendell Holmes, is one of the annalists here. She has attained two years in her tenth decade. She is hale and hearty and busy with her pen, spending much time in her little sanctum. Strict cloister life does not impair health, but rather promotes it. No one could be a better illustration of her renowned kinsman's poem entitled, 'Eighty Years and More.' In it he says:

> "At sixty-four life has begun;
> At seventy-three begin once more;
> Fly swifter as thou near'st the sun,
> And brightest shine at eighty-four,
> At ninety-five, shouldst thou survive
> Still wait on God and work and thrive.

"'Mother Holmes,' as she is familiarly called, could join hands with a sister nonagenarian of the preceding century and the latter in turn could be in close touch with Blessed Mary of the Incarnation, thus linking by some few spans the past three hundred years. So close do these years seem, that I think even the ancestors of the vegetables that we had for dinner grew under the tillage of the Foundress' busy little spade.

"A day has passed since the above was written,

and we have been to the Merici Convent, situated near the Plains of Abraham. Two of the sisters accompanied us. We visited the battle-ground, and saw the spot where Wolfe fell. A little fence surrounds it, and a slab on which is written 'Here Wolfe fell!' designates the place and the triumph of the British Flag. Mother A . . . has gathered flowers on the Plains, fertilized by the blood of heroes.

"To-morrow, we are to visit the Shrine of St. Ann de Beaupré of which you will hear later. Then we must try to sever the sweet ties that bind us to our holy sisters of Quebec and go to you who are sweeter and dearer still."

The following day Sister Mary Paul visited the shrine of St. Ann. The devotion of the pilgrims and the services at the Basilica were to her a rare spiritual tonic. Here she saw demonstrated the catechism lesson of how we must take more care of the soul than of the body. To such extent was this care of the soul carried, that the pilgrims seemed unconcerned about food, heat, discomfort, and the densely crowded Church. Quietness and brotherly thoughtfulness prevailed. It is soothing to think how hopefully things of the soul progress—now, it is Mother Mary of the Incarnation in early French Canada, then a Dom Bosco in the slums of Turin; later, heroic daughters of St. Angela in the ice-bound wildernesses of Alaska, a Sister Mary Paul in the land of sunshine and flowers. In obedience to their "Sic luceat lux vestra," these servants of God have lit up the darkness wheresoever they have carried the lamp of faith.

If struggles for the fleeting goods of life are omnipresent, so too are struggles for the soul-life. The good are marching on. They must march, because their allies are swift angels, their strongholds the desert, the wilderness, the snowy Alpine summits, and the icy fastnesses. The music of their lives is heard by those who have ears to hear, and, like the stars that dot the firmament, so do Christ's very own adorn the earth with the beauty of their activities.

But event passes event in rapid succession and our travellers are seated on the deck of the boat that is fast plying toward Montreal. Their late experiences are giving color to the moonlit St. Lawrence. The sublime language of night is sinking deep into their souls, and those to whom they had lately said adieu, seem to have imparted the peace and enjoyment that they feel amidst the soft splendors of night.

The next morning they reach Montreal, where they spend some hours with Brother Jerome of the Christian Brothers' College. This was the last halt; a farewell from Brother Jerome and the sisters turn to the West with his gracious Godspeed.

## CHAPTER X.

The Canadian Pacific Route promising its full share of scenic interest and the land of Jacques Cartier fast receding, the sisters settled themselves down to life on wheels; and O! blessed flexibility of human nature! their hearts were eager to be with their religious family notwithstanding the late pleasures which had been theirs.

Arriving at Glacier, great was the astonishment of our travellers at the stately monolith Sir Donald, which rises a naked and abrupt pyramid to the height of a mile and a quarter; near by are the glacier-fed waters of the Illecillewaet, and the Selkirk Mountains with their groups of crags so great in magnitude that eye and mind fail to grasp them. Nature here could not be personified by the appellation "Dame Nature," for femininity is of another category of natural phenomena. Some undreamed-of Titan would more fittingly answer to the yawning crevices and amazing heights. Such vast delineations, together with the Rockies, inspired the following lines:

**THE ROCKIES.**

Rockies hoary, Rockies splendid,
  Say, what are ye, things sublime?
Naught on earth proclaims the wonders
  Of God's work in any clime
As do ye, O Rocky Mountains,
  Grandest Sentinels of Time.

When Jehovah's thoughts came earthward,
  Carved He Rockies near the skies;
Chiseled them to calmest grandeur,
  Colored them in deep sunrise—
Touched their pinnacles and turrets
  In the wonders of His dyes.

O your silence, Rocky Mountains,
  Seems as if great harps had flung
All the pulsing of their anthems
  To infinity, whose tongue
Ordered silence, deep and awesome,
  Where primeval anthems rung.

Rockies, ye uphold the couches
  Whereon dies each King of Day—
Oh, the pageant of his passing!
  Oh, the pomp of your display
When you part the heaven-dyed curtains
  To admit the bier of Day.

The journey from Vancouver to San Francisco in August is attended by excessive heat, and discomfort is augmented by the crowds travelling during this season of the year. Hence it was that the trip taken by Sister Mary Paul was exhausting in the extreme, but with her usual fortitude and unselfishness, she was concerned only for her companion; and when the friendly old fog came from San Francisco Bay, she welcomed the coolness with unwonted delight.

When she reached Santa Rosa and was again in the bosom of her beloved Community, she said she would never again leave the precincts of her Convent, "unless," as she added playfully, "to take my last journey to our dear sweet Lord." In truth, the bark for this journey was at no great distance, awaiting favorable winds and a heavier cargo of spiritual goods.

In Sister M. Paul's absence, work had accumulated; but with her usual methodical way, she dispatched the accumulation by degrees till all her duties were soon again going at normal speed. She was a strong advocate of living in the present and would often quote:

> "The present, the present is all that thou hast,
> For thy sure possessing.
> Like the angel that wrestled with Jacob,
> Hold it fast till it gives thee its blessing."

The bark for her last voyage had approached nearer, and the tired voyager seemingly was destined to take passage: for she lay unconscious under a stroke of apoplexy, which gave little hope of recovery. The crisis passed, however, and almost imperceptibly at first, then more rapidly, she returned to consciousness and feebly inquired what had happened. In less than a month, she was again in her usual place reciting the Office and attending to the daily spiritual exercises.

She had so inured herself to obey the first stroke of the bell, that even in her half-conscious state, she essayed to rise the moment it rang. Reading in Christian Perfection that sickness is truthful in demonstrating one's real character, she wondered how it had revealed hers: but those who watched her returning from the portals of death saw but her spiritual beauty increased. Her solicitude had been entirely for them, lest they should be fatigued in their care of her or their sleep interrupted.

Frequently she would say, "How well we are taken care of in the house of the Lord! How sweet is His spouse, the Christian soul, to her prostrate and needy sister!" Thus her extreme unselfishness edified all in sickness as in health. The doctor gave warning that another such stroke might be fatal. Sister Mary Paul, however, thought only of the blessed union with God and repeated over and over again, "Laetatus sum in his quae dicta sunt mihi," or "Gloriosa dicta sunt de te, civitas Dei." Such joyful anticipations did but bring her back restored in health all the sooner to her eager pupils and more eager Community.

The June following her illness, elections again took place, resulting in the installation of Mother Angela as Superioress.

Order and methodical work in this régime received new and vigorous impetus, and resulted in the Ursuline College of Santa Rosa taking its place among the schools accredited to the State University, Berkeley.

To this achievement Sister M. Paul brought her best efforts and realized flattering success. Yet while she worked with the energy of former years, nevertheless a change of scene and climate being within the facilities of the sisters, was deemed expedient. Accordingly in August, she was transferred to St. Helena. Fair "Elmhurst" was all that could be desired; but fair places and salubrious climates do not fill a void in the heart. However, no hint as to interior struggles escaped Sister Mary Paul, and this new field of labor received her full attention.

From her last retreat to the day of her death, four months later, Sister Mary Paul betrayed no diminution of vigor; on the contrary, her faculties seemed more than ordinarily energized and her eagerness to do extra work became greater. Her charity became more intense as she neared the goal.

When school reopened in August, her welcome to new pupils and her renewal of friendships for old ones lost none of the warmth and enthusiasm of former occasions; nor did her usual little homily on vanity lack any of its unction by being presented in a new dress. Seeing any suggestion of powder on young faces, she would say: "Why is there so much water, if we are not to keep clean? Why is there so much air, if we are not to inhale it? Why is health of body so attractive if we do not foster it? Why is virtue so beautiful if we are not to practice it? Clean water and fresh air are nature's cosmetics and we may be as extravagant in their use as we wish."

Sometimes favorite teachers might be transferred to other departments or loved companions of pre-

Ursuline Academy, St. Helena

ceding terms might be missing, thereby leaving in childish hearts a hunger for what was. To these little sorrows she gave real sympathy or turned them aside by the humorous twinkle of her loving eyes. She deemed nothing too trifling that interfered with school happiness and she looked upon conventual training as a means of forestalling life's ills; therefore, must the Convent girl be contented in her environment, so that undisturbed and at peace she may become a builder of a personal, superior womanhood. Zeal along such lines she communicated to her co-workers. "Not only must we be efficient teachers," she would say, "but we must also be attractive ones." Things educational and intrinsically good can become dreary unless the teacher be fully alive to all the possibilities of her inestimable profession. Hospitals and prisons would dwindle in number, perhaps disappear, if women were educated to stand for all that is righteous.

The Sunday-school work of the St. Helena parish with its large class of boys had been one of her cherished occupations, because in the teaching of Christian Doctrine, the youths instructed, knowing their Master's will, will more intelligently execute it.

"They are most tenderly human who have gone deepest into the divine," says the Poet-priest. Thus we find Sister Mary Paul looking eagerly for Santa Rosa letters and she did not allow work to hinder her correspondence.

Among letters especially dear to her were found the following lines from her friend M. A.:

"Euntes Ibant et Flebant Mittentes Semina Sua, Venientes autem Venient cum Exultation, Portantes Manipulos Suos."

    Far, far away to a distant land,
    I sent my love with a radiant band,
    Of other loves, that they might sow
    In marshes low
    The goodly seed.

    Ah me! they went their way and wept,
    And all along that land storm-swept,
    On virgin soil they cast the seed
    And plucked the weed,
    To succor crop.

    In their new land, a Love supreme
    Uplifted them on am'rous theme,
    Till hardest toil seemed naught but pleasure,
    For am'rous treasure
    Them repaid.

    O, love of mine, in your bleak land,
    Toil on, till life's great sphere of sand
    Runs through the isthmus of its glass—
    For weeds, alas!
    Abound for aye.

    In your far land, O love of mine,
    Await your sheaves; lo! Christ Divine
    Is rip'ning them to golden strands—
    And angel bands,
    Your allies are.

And why should not spiritual fructification take place where such seeds were sown, where such approved tillage went on daily, where such a laborer was hourly afield, singing in her heart her dominant note—"Ad majorem Dei gloriam"?

Intense application to every detail of her duty was beginning to tell on her vitality; and when warned that she must relax a little, she pleaded that one year of vigorous service given to our dear Lord was worth a dozen in which physical cares were so noticed that the soul lost much of its tranquillity and activity. It was God's will that she should stay yet a little while to burn the dross of imperfection and so bring forth genuine metal.

The more surely to accomplish this, she was called by the usual annual retreat into the "Desert" for the last time, to "hide in the hollow places of the rocks" with Jesus, the Lord of the desert. In this particular retreat He was preparing her soul to meet Him. As has been said the interim between this retreat and the death of Sister M. Paul was but a few months.

Reverend Father Mackay, S. J., directed the retreat of 1912, and being encouraged spiritually in the ways and means she was using, Sister Mary Paul came forth with unwonted exaltation of spirit. "How I should love to go to our dear Lord, now that I am entirely ready!" she was heard to say—the word "entirely" signifying the manner in which she had applied the Exercises to her own needs in the event of a near summons; for it must be borne in mind that from the first stroke of apoplexy, she had an abiding presentiment that another would prove fatal.

A sister companion of Sister Mary Paul in this retreat has contributed the following:

In the unitive phase of retreat with the celerity with which a released stone flies to the mark intended, so flew the soul of Sister Mary Paul to the Center of her soul's repose.

She, whose first fervor had never relaxed, took renewed resolution to love our Lord and to cause Him to be loved to the extent that future effort in her ebbing tide of mortal existence would permit.

Sister Mary Paul, as has been mentioned elsewhere, who had asked a sister why she wept and the Spouse so near, and, later seeing a sister sorely afflicted at the sight of death, inquired why she was so affected—this child of smiles and laughter, she, an alien to tears, struggled with them in her last retreat. The throes of nature in the combat of complete surrender come to most persons in the face of impending death, but in her case they were tears of devotion, not of grief. She was proverbially a cheerful giver, and the "Ecce quam bonum" of the hour of renovation at the close of retreat found her restored to her usual buoyancy. Nature's "fitful fever" had been checked forever in this her last retreat.

# CHAPTER XI.

We have now but to follow our loved sister a few paces more. Her lamp is trimmed. She is near the door. The Bridegroom's Hand is upon the latch, and lo! she soon will listen to the "Bridal Bells of Veni, Sponsa Christi."

Time was climbing apace and November, the sweetly sad month of the Poor Souls had come, bringing with it the feast of St. Stanislaus Kotska. He was one of Sister Mary Paul's favorite saints, and though we know little as to how our heavenly friends are actuated towards us, except that they act for our good, we may yet piously believe that they are permitted by God to have accidental joys regarding us. St. Stanislaus rejoiced when on his Feast, November 13th, he placed his client on the some time stern spot, which we call threshold. Here the Master found her with all her work finished. She was in readiness to give an account of her stewardship.

St. Aloysius being asked what he would wish to be doing, were he called from life within the recreation hour, replied, "I would wish to be playing this game, because I began it through obedience and therefore I am pleasing God." In like manner, did Sister Mary Paul acquit herself of her work on the 13th of November, and its close found her performing to the letter what obedience had been requiring. Since "the obedient man shall speak of victory," so also will she for all eternity. Victory was in the day's spiritual service, victory was in the exhortation which she had given M. F. of Calistoga, an exhortation which completed her religious work among the children and, needless to say, this last advice was, and ever will be, cherished by the recipient. School work had received no less attention from this faithful custodian of the class-room. Everything had been prepared for the morrow—papers corrected and graded and school work arranged. Altar-breads had been left ready at her hand for the morning's Sacrifice. Sister Mary Paul's work was done, and done well; her prayers had been said, her sheaves gathered, and St. Stanislaus was begging her speedy entrance to the realm of saints. The Spoiler came. The world of sense was fast wheeling into darkness, leaving her only time to call for help.

On many occasions during her religious life did she express the desire that God might send the friend of her heart to assist her when death came. Answering the call for help, this friend hastened to console her in the few conscious moments left. Sister Mary Paul received the last Sacraments, and pillowed on her friend's strong arm, she sank into deep unconsciousness wherein the voice of friendship could no longer penetrate; nor could the hand of friendship perform aught that could rob the weary hours of death's portentous calm.

As the clock marked the moment when, in the decrees of God, the sufferer should hear the words: "Come! my love, the rains are over, the winter is gone!" she stirred not in body but her spirit went forth to obey His invitation. To those who prayed

# Life of Sister Mary Paul of the Cross

beside her, she seemed to have passed from a troubled dream into a tranquil sleep; her shapely head framed itself in its pillow, her small delicate hands lay on the coverlet, her features, relaxing from the brain pressure of the past eighteen hours, assumed the expression of imperturbable peace, and Sister Mary Paul was lost to this world.

She had left from New York to California a trail of goodness—hardened hearts softened, bad habits changed to good, occasions of sin deserted; new means of saving souls set working, neighbors at variance united: this was the grand spiritual scenery along the trail of this high-souled servant of God—"Their works follow them."

And you, who observe the fulfillment of a dutiful life, kneel at the bier of Sister Mary Paul and see how glorious is the law of compensation in the religious world. For the one whom she might have influenced, as votary of the world, thousands are influenced by her, as the votary of religion; for was she not panoplied by God and by the great Order in which she had served Him? Had she not tasted how sweet it is to serve, and tasting, did she not lure others to the banquet?

The last rites over, Sister Mary Paul's remains were placed in the grave beside Mother Alphonse Costella. Between the interments of these two a whole generation had intervened.

Prior to the death of Mother Alphonse, a new cemetery had been purchased by Saint Rose's parish and Mother Alphonse was one of the first to be interred therein. At that time, there was a holy rivalry as to which plot should be nearest the Sisters; but at Sister Mary Paul's interment, so thickly settled had become this portion of God's acre, that no rivalry was needed. However, sad hearts crowded the "green hillside," eager to behold the casket wherein lay the beloved form of the dead. Amidst tears and sobs, dust was consigned to dust, and the Maker of all held sway with that blessed calm which turns sorrow into resignation and the sense of loss into hope of reunion in the Kingdom of God.

Truly did Sister Mary Paul become one of our Faithful Departed, for she testified it by the favors she obtained for the loved ones of her immediate family as well as for those of her spiritual one. May she, in her long sleep in Calvary cemetery of Santa Rosa, be ever a quiet sentinel to those, who in her lifetime were wont to say that her admonition regarding the omission of a Mass or any sacred duty, was urging them to be faithful, whenever temptation to repeat these serious faults presented themselves.

Her charity will not be lessened in heaven for, enlightened by love, our sweet Mother Mary and the heavenly inhabitants will be love's allies, and the work begun upon earth by this holy Ursuline will be continued in powerful impetration. "Those who instruct others unto justice, shall shine as stars for all eternity!" best expresses the apotheosis of the Apostolate of Education to which, as Ursuline Sister, she was called.

View of Walk Approaching the Convent.

Following is a tribute taken from the Santa Rosa Press Democrat:

"Mother Paul of Ursuline College Called to Rest.

"Into the bright sunshine of the Eternal life the soul of sainted Mother Paul, for over forty years a Sister of the Ursuline Community, and for over thirty years connected with Ursuline College in this city, passed away on Thursday afternoon at five o'clock. She died at Elmhurst Academy, a branch of Ursuline College at St. Helena, where she had been for some time.

"Not only will Mother Paul's death be a sad blow to those who have been associated with her for many years in the devoted work of the Ursuline Order, but also are there hundreds of men, women, and children, who, having come under her kindly influence—for kinder soul never lived—will learn of her passing with sincere sorrow. She was idolized by the hundreds who during the years have been students at the Ursuline College. A number of Santa Rosa's prominent Catholic men learned their first lessons at the school with Mother Paul as instructor in the Boys' School, a department work at the College. In after life they never lost their love and regard for her. She was always glad to see the pupils of former years return to their Alma Mater in the dignity of motherhood and the exaltation of true womanhood.

"Mother Paul was a charming woman, one whom it was always a pleasure to meet. She had a remarkably sweet disposition and a concern for the well-being of others. She loved to be in active service in the College faculty and management, and no task was allotted to her but what was happily performed. Her influence for good has gone far and wide, and of her it can be truthfully said in the words of the Scriptures:

"'Blessed are the dead who die in the Lord, even so, for they rest from labors and their works do follow them.'

"In the world prior to assuming the veil of the Ursuline Sisterhood Mother Paul was Miss Margaret Morrissey. She came of an old and distinguished New York family. She is survived by several relatives. One brother is City Engineer Morrissey of Dunkirk, New York. The Rev. Father J. M. Cassin, rector of St. Rose's Church and pastor of the deceased for the past twenty-two years, sent him a telegram Thursday night informing him of his sister's death. Rev. Father Cassin paid Mother Paul a splendid tribute Thursday night in discussing her life work.

"Mother Superioress Angela and Sister U . . . will accompany the remains of Mother Paul to this city today, and the funeral will take place from the Church of St. Rose to-morrow morning. There will be a Solemn Requiem High Mass, celebrated for the repose of her soul by Reverend Father Cassin, assisted by four other priests and the interment will be in Calvary cemetery in the plot specially set aside for the Ursuline Community. Mother Paul is the first Sister of the Community to die here in twenty-five years, the last being Mother Alphonse."

## IN MEMORIAM.

(From the "Boston Pilot.")

### A PERFECT DAY.

Ay, but the day was passing fair;
  Descendant of some sweet Spring,
Sent out by God through wintry air,
  A lily-white soul to bring—

A veiled sanctity she lay
  In deep eternal rest.
Bright angels led her soul away;
  Bright joy her soul caressed.

O love, O clasp of Jesus' Hand!
  O Rest on the Savior's Breast!
O wondrous view of the Promised Land!!
  O joy to be one of its blest!

Thy life was a perfect day, O Nun:
  Thy Master's work complete—
What rapture when His grand, "Well done!"
  Made thy heaven with joy replete.

So rare a gem thou ill couldst spare,
  O Earth, that hast so few—
Will angel hands with loving care
  Shape other gems for you?

O lift your jewel casket, Earth,
  Therein will Christ replace
The gem He took, nor fear a dearth
  Among His shining race.

Another tribute from the San Francisco Monitor:

"THE END OF A PERFECT DAY.

"Thursday at Elmhurst Academy, St. Helena, as the autumn sun slowly sinking over the western hills of Napa, blazoned their vine-covered slopes with the golden glow of evening, the gentle spirit of Mother Mary Paul passed into the light of God's eternal day. But a few moments before in the full enjoyment of health, she knelt in loving adoration before our Divine Lord in the Most Blessed Sacrament and His summons seemed an answer to her rapturous prayer. An ecstatic smile illumined the dying countenance as though at the close of a perfect day her eager soul already beheld the glory of the Lord.

"Miss Margaret Morrissey, in religion Sister Mary Paul, entered the Ursuline order thirty-five years ago and was one of the zealous nuns that one year later left the Mother House of the Ursulines, St. Martins, Brown County, Ohio, to found at Santa Rosa in distant California the first convent of the Order west of the mountains.

"Like the pioneer of the Ursulines in America, Mother Mary of the Incarnation, whose name is inseparably linked with the early heroic history of Canada, these devoted Sisters left friends and associations dear to them that they might aid in teaching the mystic beauties of faith to a land that dreamed only of gold.

"One of a gifted family, Mother Mary Paul had received an excellent education. She was a mathematician of marked ability and was well versed in Latin and other languages. For many years she taught these subjects to the senior classes at Ursuline College.

"From the beginning, as teacher in the parochial school, Mother Mary Paul was intimately connected with the parish of St. Rose, and many men and women to-day owe what is best in them to the early training received from her. Others, too, knew the benefit of her kindly counsel: no throbbing heart, no aching brain appealed in vain to Mother Paul. Of her it may be truly said:

"The tidal wave of deeper souls
Into our inmost being rolls.
And lifts one unawares
Out of all meaner cares.

"Several years ago Mother Paul suffered a stroke of paralysis from which, however, she completely recovered and she had been engaged in active work at Elmhurst Academy for some time previous to her death.

"Rev. Mother Superior Angela, Rev. Mother Agatha, and Sister E. . . . escorted the casket from St. Helena to Santa Rosa where the mortal form surrounded by love's last offering, beautiful flowers, lay in St. Rose's Church until Saturday morning. A Requiem high Mass was celebrated at that time by Rev. John M. Cassin, rector of the parish, assisted by Rev. Father Casey of San Francisco, Rev. Father Fletcher of Petaluma, Rev. Maurice Barry, Cloverdale, and Rev. John R. Cantillon of Sebastopol. The Sisters' choir of Ursuline College rendered the music, and Miss Anna Smith of Cloverdale, a former pupil of Mother Paul, presided at the organ.

"Rev. Father Cassin spoke of the noble work done by Mother Mary Paul for many years in the parish and eulogized the spirit that, obedient to the higher call, did great things for God. 'Other women,' he said, 'have wrought wondrous beauty in silver and gold and marble, but Mother Mary Paul molded immortal souls.' Father Cassin referred touchingly to the kindly heart of one well worthy to rank in the great army of Catholic Sisterhoods, the noblest the world will ever know.

"As the casket was reverently borne from the altar of that God whom she had long served so faithfully and lovingly in the land of the living, voices vibrant with emotion poured forth the words, 'And Thou, O Jesus, Art All Mine.' In the distance, the bell of St. Ursula's chapel tolled a mournful farewell from Sister associates, who while life lasts will cherish the memory of Mother Mary Paul: for 'the just shall be in everlasting remembrance: [she] shall not be afraid for any evil report.'"

## LETTERS WRITTEN BY SISTER MARY PAUL.

Dear ——

A most happy Feast! May it be a foretaste of the beautiful heavenly Feast towards which we are making such strides! Who listened with joy and executed with **exultant joy** the command of the Master, when He said, "Go forth from thy father's house into a strange land"? who, but you ——, our "Angel of Napa Valley!"

For many years, sweet imitator of St. Theresa, you have lifted up to the unthinking world the snowy banners of your march heavenwards and bravely you have marched under the leadership of your Divine Captain. With poverty, chastity, and obedience emblazoned on your shield, march on with your Leader, Christ, the most beautiful among the sons of men! He will show you the direct way, and He has in His loving care the reward of your labors. How often has your banner inspired me to reach for things that cannot perish! Away up in the distance I think I hear, "Veni Sponsa Christi" urging you and me to make haste. What a crown He intends to lay on the head of His Spouse, who on October 15, 1912, will have offered to Him the merits of so many years. May the holy Angels keep you, an earthly angel, in all your ways and may my poor prayers obtain for you an increase of grace and love of God! I have you down in the "Round Tower of my heart and there I shall keep you forever and a day," so do not try to escape even though you are so detached from human ties.

Your loving Sister,
SISTER MARY PAUL.

Dear J ——

You will be glad to hear that Mother Superior has sent me to St. Helena for a few days' rest. I came over with three of the children, who are to remain during the vacation; one however, expects to go home for part of the free time. There are only two Sisters over here now, Sisters A . . . and F . . ., and Mother will send for me just as soon as she receives definite word regarding the annual retreat. Just to think one whole year has flown past since Mother and I were travelling east, and oh! what a glorious trip that was! Perhaps God made it such in preparation for the crosses awaiting dear Mother's return.

The Sisters who were ill the same time that I was, are quite well now, but I think that they will never be strong. It is just as well, however, as it makes us reflect that we have not here a lasting City. I never realized the fleetness of time so much as I do now. Time is only a short period of probation given us to prepare for our true life in Eternity.

God bless you all and keep you free from the contamination of this wicked world. Soon we shall meet in Heaven. "In Heaven we know our own."

Do not worry about darling M. She will get stronger when she finishes her growth. Are you not consoled by the fact that she is an angel in human form? May she remain so till she takes her flight to the Bosom of God!

To-day is a Western holiday, the Admission Day of our golden State into the Union. I am delighted to spend a part of it with those whom I love next to God and my dear community.

I received dear K's letter. It made my heart rejoice as do all her letters, because they are so much like J's. They tell me just what I desire most to know—that all my dear ones are well and also what each is doing.

I am delighted to know that you all saw Mother A's relatives in Rochester, especially Rev. Father N. I hope that dear J. will see him often and become one of his bosom friends. Clerical friends if true to their high calling in all respects, are treasures which neither gold nor influence can purchase.

For the past three days there has been a Vintage Festival in St. Helena. Our graduate, Miss F . . ., a beautiful Italian, has been chosen Queen. This gracious Queen was inspired to call on the Sisters. Accordingly, yesterday in response to the door-bell ring, the sister opening the door was greeted by a handsome courtier, an attendant of the Queen, saying, "The Queen wishes to pay her respects to the Sisters." Presto! a number of autos appeared on the grounds. Mother went down the steps to the royal equipage and saluted the Queen and her court. Queen Inez was every inch a Queen—nature's Queen and an excellent Catholic one.

At 10:30 A. M. the pageant will pass by the Convent along Main Street. It will be three miles long. Strange, dear people, that we left the world for God, and yet how much of the beautiful does not that same God show us without our leaving the grounds.

I will be glad if dear J. and K. live in R. It is a beautiful City Think well before you make a change, for you know that J's high position is not lasting, and even were it permanent, my dear princely brother cannot stand many more years of such strenuous work, notwithstanding he looks so well. No doubt this is due to his pure and upright living with the love and tenderness of the best of wives and the consolation of the most charming of children.

Your loving sister,

S. M. P.

Thursday, May 25, 1899.

Dearest Mother:

What an exciting day this is at home, and what adjective can fully describe to-night! Children, parents, friends—all gathered for a few hours in the assembly hall of the College to enjoy and to bear testimony to the great work of the Sisters, God's holy workers.

A few hours, then an empty hall, but each occupant

has taken with him or her a something, he knows not what, that will bear fruit. He will cast a grateful glance back to the vacant hall situated as it is under the dear Chapel where The Master from the Tabernacle ever watches those who come and go; and He blesses most those who love the sisters best.

D . . . arrived between 1 and 1:30 P. M. He looked fatigued, so did "Duke," the best of horses. We unpacked the sweet-faced statue of our Blessed Mother. How kind of you to think of sending it just now, during the whirlpool of excitement incident to the closing of school! The statue is already in the chapel on its neat pedestal: on each side of the statue I placed a vase of beautiful La France and Lamarck roses and in front, two fancy candlesticks.

To-night **we** shall have our May devotions near that same dear statue before which you have so often knelt; but to-night, **you,** surrounded by many strangers, will be in St. Ursula's Hall: shall we forget you and fail to pray for your success? Even though we should do so, our blessed Mother will not.

Lovingly,
SISTER M. PAUL.

---

Santa Rosa, November 23, 1899.

My fond B . . .

Congratulations in the new state of life upon which you have entered! May the Divine Master, who was present at your joyous nuptials and who received through His holy representative, the dear officiating Passionist, your sacred contract, remain ever with you and yours by His holy presence, making you an Angel of peace, of comfort, and of consolation over your household, and may He give you a foretaste of that happiness awaiting you in the life to come!

It was a joy to me to learn that you were married in dear St. Mary's, the sacred church of our tender years:

and what renders it more sacred is the fact that there took place the holy and solemn rites over our dear saintly father, whose noble example you are so carefully following.

How consoling that our dear good brother J. was with you! I think often of each one of you and marvel at the tenderness of our heavenly Father in keeping you all together. Our saintly mother must be the holy magnet which attracts all our loved ones in or near Dunkirk.

I hope that some day you will come to the Golden West to see the sister who so loves and venerates each fond brother and dear sister and who cherishes an intense veneration for our sweet mother. How proud she must have felt to see you married in the Church which she visits so often! I will pray often for you, dear brother, and I desire that your life be one of sunshine.

Please write me a Xmas letter.

Again extending to you my warmest congratulations and hoping to see you before I die,

Your loving sister,

S. M. P.

---

Santa Rosa, April 19, 1900.

Dear J . . ..

I received the Utica "News" containing your photo just as I was looking forward to an Easter letter from you. I find you changed but it would not be natural were it not so. Your features bear the same look that characterized your boyhood, and now that you have grown into noble manhood and have grave responsibilities not only to your own but also to your fellow men, and especially that you have acquitted yourself very well, I am delighted and proud of my dear brother. The paper states that you are the most popular of City Officials. Thank God! My greatest delight is that I know you have gained that popularity (am I not right?) by purity and uprightness of conduct. These are means that will make you not only popular amongst men, but also among the saints of God whose company you will one day join with your fond and loving wife, your saintly mother and all your fond brothers and sisters, not forgetting our dear sainted father, whose footsteps you are so bravely following. Yes; dear brother, you are not called to the priesthood, but you can be an apostle; for the silent influence of good example will be powerful among those non-Catholic friends of yours. An old pagan philosopher whose writings still live, says that, "words persuade, but example draws."

I will not forget you in my prayers on the feast of your patron and mine, Saint Paul of the Cross. . . .

Devotedly,

S. M. P.

---

Sunday, May 31, 1903.

My fond B . . .

Last Friday your long, kind and most welcome letter was received. It was written on May 4th, which date is sacred to me, as it is the anniversary of my holy profession. This fact not only added joy to the receipt of your letter but also a tenderness which only sacred memories can recall.

So God has blessed you with another little angel! God bless him and make him, if possible, a greater man than his father! I am delighted to learn that you have called him James Paul. St. Paul of the Cross will have one more client added to his list. Be thankful to Almighty God for all His special favors and graces to the Morrissey family. To you He has been most kind in giving you so gentle, so loving, and so genial a companion. Be kind to her at all times. I cannot imagine you, dear J., anything else but benevolent. Still, you may be blessed with a long life, and no life is free from trials and contradictions, which are designedly Godsends, as tests of our metal in the crucible of endurance, and also reminders to us that we are made for Heaven.

The two darlings which make your heart rejoice are lent to you, not given, and some day you must return them to God who created them for Heaven.

Do not be troubled. Those court decisions are annoying but make every day an invocation to our Lady of Good Counsel, then say what you think and God will take care of the issue. "Our Lady of Good Counsel, pray for me," is a short but efficacious aspiration. Say it often and note results. Will it tax you too much if I request you to learn that short "Memorare of St. Bernard"? In times of pressing business and annoying circumstances, it may be the only special prayer that you will have time to say. But say it, no matter how hard the trial may be; it will bring you a rich reward.

You cannot feel more delighted than I to know that you are in your new home. It must be a Paradise on earth. I remember the location well. Everything about it was pleasing to me. I did not see the interior but the exterior speaks for it. You told me it had every modern improvement, so I can imagine how commodious and convenient it is. Thank God! You must not regret that I did not see it. My visit among you remains without a flaw to mar its joy.

You gave me such a beautiful account of all the dear ones at home that I cannot express in words my gratitude: the heart speaks and feels a language that words cannot express. Dear M . . ., what a comfort, what a mother she has been to us all! And dear J . . ., is there not something in him far above the ordinary? There is something in the name John: it means the gracious gift of God. It was John, our Lord's gift to His own Mother on Calvary's mount, who stood by the Cross with Mary, our Immaculate Mother, when the other Apostles had fled: so, too, my dearest brother watched the closing moments of our saintly mother and still remains with the other fond ones in the old homestead. Time is fleeting. Soon it will be no more. Then will Eternity unfold before us and we shall be again reunited never more to know pain or parting.

Try to hear holy Mass on the 25th prox. Last year I had the great pleasure of hearing it with you and offering my Holy Communion for you, a favor I never thought would have been granted me. God is so good and His merciful ways manifold.

Your loving sister,<br>
S. M. P.

---

My dear ones:

To-morrow evening we shall begin our annual retreat and your devoted sister cannot permit the day to pass without sending you one and all a few loving lines. Reverend Father S., S. J., has been appointed to conduct the exercises of retreat.

To-day is Reverend Father C's birthday. He is sixty-four and as active as a young priest, notwithstanding his many and arduous labors in the Master's vineyard. We are having a little celebration in his honor.

The Sisters from St. Helena have come home for retreat.

Yesterday Mother A. went over to St. Helena with two sisters, who are to remain during the retreat, Sisters M. M. and P., the latter Mother's cousin. Mother invited me to take the drive over with her, but I told her that I was afraid she would leave me there and so deprive me of the retreat. Mother laughed, and so I am here in dear Santa Rosa full of unmolested and delightful anticipation.

I often think of dear little M . . . and wonder if by the solemn act of religious Profession she will ever be a Spouse of our dear Lord. If I could convince her of the sweets of the sacrificial life that God has bestowed on your fond sister, how earnestly would I plead to have her come to California, the land of sunshine and flowers.

I have been under the most prudent and the most kind-hearted of Superiors. Mother A . . . goes out of office this month: were she not so fatigued and in need of rest from so onerous a responsibility, I think we would ask to have her re-elected. Please to tell darling M . . . that I think we shall never get another Mother A . . .; still, if M . . . gives herself to Almighty God without reserve, not looking for perfection in this vale of tears, God will supply in her regard another such mother in prudence and tenderness and rightmindedness, which virtues are rare and God-given.

      Devotedly,
          S. M. P.

---

Dear . . .

Now I shall travel to 30 W. 4th Street. J . . . is at home. O dear gentle K . . . and noble J . . . How are you both? Well, thank God, and fonder of each other than ever, and here's holy dignified M . . .! This paragraph is jaunty, is it not?

Now I must sermonize. Remember, dear brother, you cannot keep the Faith untarnished in this materialistic and socialistic age without the constant weapon of daily prayer.

Mother has just been called over to Santa Rosa to see Rev. Father Casey who is going to dear old Ireland to visit his home. I feel Mother's going just as much as I did when at home with you on my trip; Mother went to Rochester; you remember? And I so longed for her return? I cannot tell you, dear people, what a tender mother she has been to me all during my long religious life. God was merciful to me to send me to a convent where such a noble woman was Superior. May our dear sweet Lord send to darling M . . . such another, when God calls the child to be His chosen Spouse.

This last scholastic year in St. Helena (if I may make a comparison) has been marked with God's special blessing and tenderness, a year of holy loving peace. Our Convent here is nestled among the foothills of the Coast

Range; this year dear Mother A . . . has been our guiding star, and the St. Helenaites are happy to be under her fostering care.

With love,

S. M. P.

---

Feb. 22, 1911.

My own beloved sister:

As this is a holiday I can spend a part of the time with you. We often speak of our wonderful trip East, and the pleasure we experienced in meeting our dear ones. God bless and keep them in good health and spirits!

When I want to have a good laugh, I recall to my mind the photo which represents my dear sweet L., looking up with closed eyes! (An Irish Bull.) Doesn't she look comical?

Please to tell dear J . . . that his watch is keeping excellent time. I have permission to use it, and I find it a great convenience, especially in timing my spiritual reading and in making connections from one duty to another. May God bless J. and keep him holy. I send the Passionist Fathers now and then a postal, picturing some beautiful natural scenery of California. Thus do I honor dear Reverend Father Hugh Barr of blessed memory and dear Father Peter whose kindness to our saintly mother is always remembered.

Enclosed you will find a clipping from the Santa Rosa "Press Democrat." The young priest of whom the paper writes, Rev. J. T. . . ., C. S. P., was one of our pupils. He says that when I prepared him for Confirmation I gave him the honor of reading the Act of Renewal of Baptismal Promises. We are proud of him. As a little boy we noticed he was above the ordinary; hence Mother A . . . advised him to go to College, which he did, and now he has heard the "Tu es Sacerdos" and he promises great things in his holy calling.

S. M. P.

The little Margery so often mentioned in the letters of Sister Mary Paul, since the demise of her beloved aunt, has written the following, which may be of interest in demonstrating how prayers are answered, piety instilled, and aspirations for the religious life fostered:

Dear Mother A.:

Last Thursday was my fifteenth birthday and you know that I want to go to the convent when I am sixteen. I feel as though I could not stay in this world a single day after June First, 1916. Please to write and tell me all about the Ursulines.

Last Sunday evening we had a procession and May-crowning in our Church. This evening they are to have another procession to celebrate Corpus Christi. Five of our children will take part in both. . . .

I was obliged to stop writing last night and go to the procession; so I waited until after school to-day to finish this letter. The procession was very beautiful.

Examinations come next week. I take English, Algebra, German, Biology, Writing, and Drawing. I have little time to myself these days. I am obliged to practice an hour daily on the piano.

Aunt S. sent me the Autobiography of the Little Flower of Jesus and I have become greatly interested in her.

Lovingly yours,
MARGERY.

---

St. Helena, Easter Monday, April 3, 1899.

To the dear Sisters in Santa Rosa:

I tender heartfelt Easter greetings to each of my dear sisters, as if named, and trust that the angelic strains of the Pascal season will be ever audible till "the day dawn and the morning star rise." We are all well and grateful to you for sending our beloved Mother for Easter. Your sacrifice, dear Sisters, was among our Easter joys, and I will not say how Mother has enjoyed the trip. Let the account from her own unselfish lips be your reward.

On Holy Saturday we had Mass in the convent. Reverend Father R . . ., S. J., was assisting Reverend Father B . . ., hence, to our spiritual delight we had Easter by anticipation in our chapel. Reverend Father R . . . called to see us and seemed pleased to meet us here.

On Palm Sunday the Parish Church was beautifully and lavishly decorated. It was a small reminder of the entrance into Jerusalem. The Sanctuary foliage comprised large feathery palms eight and nine feet high, magnolia branches, and long lacy branches of the olive tree. One could almost see the meek and lowly Jesus riding through them. Then came the sad thought of fickle man, who in a few days after so grand a display, changed their words of praise to words of condemnation. At the Three Hours' Agony on Good Friday I prayed for all your intentions.

Since the rain, Elmhurst is more beautiful than ever. The trees and flowers and shrubs and vines, each with its peculiar coloring, shape and size, bears the impress of the Master's Almighty Hand.

I will not tell you anything about the school as Mother will tell you everything. Dear Father C. sent us a pretty postal with the season's cheery Alleluias.

Your affectionate sister, in our Lord,
SISTER M. PAUL.

---

My dear Brother J . . .

I have just finished re-reading the clipping from the Evening Observer which came to-day—"Honor for Dunkirk Man."

May God protect and bless you! How delighted your saintly mother and father would be, had they the happiness of seeing their son J., so exalted in the minds and hearts of the people.

They look down upon you from their high throne in

Heaven and rejoice with me and all our loved ones. I remember you in dear old Sheridan Center; as children, we wanted you to be a priest of God, but that special honor I trust is reserved for your precious darlings. May God give them the sublime vocation of being called to the priesthood, is the ardent desire of your loving sister in far California. You my dear brother are a priest in your good and holy life, but not of God's Anointed. You are now a member of the A. S. C. E. How did you win that honor? You won it not only through the public acknowledgment of your justly merited work but also by the purity and uprightness of your conduct.

Continue, dear brother, to work like a priest among your non-Catholic friends and teach them by your silent, pure, and noble life the ways of God. No wonder, dear J., you are rising on the ladder of fame with two Mothers in Heaven. Did not our earthly mother receive you from our heavenly Mother on the glorious Feast of Her Assumption into Heaven? May my dear brother rise on the ladder of perfection till he reach the Bosom of God where he will rest for all Eternity!

Lovingly,
S. M. P.

In connection with the Jubilee trip of Sr. Mary Paul, the following "Welcome" was received from St. Martins:

My dear Sister A . . .

At last! at last! I reach my arms to you and yours across the hills and valleys of the old Ohio State, and bid you welcome to Brown Co.! Welcome home! and indeed if you had brought your whole Community of Santa Rosa, we would find room for them! We are all impatience to have you. I enclose some postals and letters that have come for you, so I felt sure you must have fully decided to come. I have written to Oak St., that you will be there on Sunday, and I hope you will write and let Sister Fidelis know by what train you will come in, so that they may have some one meet you at the depot. You will find at Oak St., some that you know well, Sisters Gonzaga, Helena, John Berchmans, Louise, Alexis, and Angela. I will write Sister F . . . myself to await your coming.

I expect to take solid comfort out of your visit. Sister Helena has just heard of the death of her brother, Dr. Frank Hines.

Now, my dear Sister, au revoir! We shall await you with impatience.

Devotedly,

S. M.

---

Santa Rosa, Aug. 15, 1909.

A thrice happy birthday, my dear brother J. What a gift you were to our dear parents! Surely our blessed Mother wished to endow them with something worthy of her grand feast, and behold! she made them rejoice, because a son was "born into the world!" Your birthday comes on a day that makes us forget that our heavenly Mother bears the title of Mater Dolorosa, because the Assumpta est Maria, reiterated in the day's office makes us think only of her glories.

To-day Mother has gone to St. Helena on a sad mission; namely, to bring back with her Sister A . . . whose father, a Santa Rosa resident, has just passed into the Home of the blessed. On the day of his burial the Sisters' Choir will sing the Requiem, a consolation for the bereaved family, who like you, my dear people, have given a member to our Lord to the religious life.

So many wayside graces come to the consecrated spouses of Christ that we are carried, so to speak, trustfully in His Arms, and our relatives share in our consolations and heavenly favors. May He bless you forever and ever.

Devotedly,

Santa Rosa, Feb. 1909.

My darling little M.:

You shall have a letter all to yourself. God bless and keep you all for Himself! I was glad to hear that you all had your throats blessed on the feast of St. Blase. Rev. Father C. came over to the Convent and we had the same blessing from his consecrated hands.

How are papa and mama spending the winter? I hope they are free from colds. And how are your brothers? I can see them all so distinctly, especially brave little T. May the Divine Infant Jesus guard and protect them all from the influence of this wicked world and make them dear to Himself and to His saints!

Do not study too hard, because I want my little M. to be very strong when she comes to California to take her aunt's place! Your parents and brothers will then come to see their darling where sunshine, flowers, birds, trees, and the best humored weather exist, and you will be seen amid trees and flowers going forward to meet them. A virginal veil will be on your head, and you will be the sweetest little Ursuline in all the world. Pray for this, my darling, and for

Your loving aunt,
SISTER M. PAUL.

---

Darling little M.:

Your postal from the North Pole came just as you said it would, on Xmas Eve. Did you break the record of Peary and go nearer the Pole?

Your father tells me that you want to be a nun and come to California to our charming convent. God bless you darling, and may you realize the granting of this holy wish! Shall I tell you how to be a nun even now? Very well, listen attentively, and put into practice whatever you hear of good, and then you will be like a nun even before you come to California. Love papa and mama so much that you will never disobey them, then you will be obedient like a real nun. Be gentle and kind to your brothers; being older than they, you must be to them a visible Guardian Angel, always speaking the truth and now and again taking them to St. Mary's and kneeling with them very close to the altar where Jesus awaits you and them. He will bless and strengthen you. Again you will be like a nun. Be polite to your schoolmates and choose for companions only those whom mama and papa approve. Be attentive and submissive to all your teachers, then M. will be like a nun. There are duties that you will find easy when you practice them often and this practice will prepare you for being a real nun in beautiful California.

Ask your dear Aunt M. and Uncle J. to bring you often to St. Mary's because you want to ask Jesus in the Blessed Sacrament for many graces for papa and mama and all your relatives, and you know He will hear all your prayers and grant your requests, provided the petitions are for the good of those for whom you pray. Sometimes pray that your dear little brothers will become priests.

Again, may the Divine Infant Jesus and His Mother bless you all.

Devotedly,

S. M. P.

---

Santa Rosa, Aug. 15, 1909.

My dear E.:

Just a few lines on this great Feast of our Immaculate Mother to tell you that I was delighted with the sentiments of your last sweet letter. Let us thank God that my dear E. is becoming just what I want her to become. Continue to receive Holy Communion, for you know that Holy Communion is called "the wine that bringeth forth virgins."

I hope that after the "fret and fever" of a few years you will hear from the Divine Lips of our dear Lord, "Well done, thou good and faithful servant, enter thou into the joy of Thy Lord." Be good, be a hearer of Mass, be cautious, be a child of prayer, and all things will turn out for your good. It is very easy to be influenced by the "crowd"; but when sickness, old age, or some accident befalls one, then it is that the "crowd" proves useless, but the strength that one has acquired in keeping God's law, will be an abiding comfort.

We as Catholics have noble, defined principles, and we must live up to them no matter what may be the practice of the jostling crowd. "Time is short and Eternity long." Enjoy life but with moderation. "We have not here a lasting city, but seek we one that is to come."

I will often pray for my dear E. and whenever she visits Santa Rosa, a warm, motherly welcome awaits her
From her most affectionate,
SR. M. PAUL.

Ursuline Academy, Feb. 6, 1910.
My dear E.:

Your sweet and welcome letter gave me much pleasure. I am delighted that our Ursuline postal gave you so much consolation. I knew that it would recall to my dear E. many pleasing recollections. When do you think we will see you again at "Ursuline"?

Wednesday next will begin the holy "Season of Lent." Do not fast too rigorously, dear E. Let your confessor direct your fast.

St. John Berchmans was asked once what devotion was most pleasing to the Mother of God: he answered, any devotion no matter how small, provided it be constant. Constancy, dear E., that is the secret of success. You must determine on one day of the week, or even two, on which you will go to Mass and be faithful to the determination. Then, do not multiply prayers, but be more devout in those that you daily say. By doing this, you will not fatigue the mind and you will be constant with intensity modified, but not diminished.

I wish you to take good care of yourself as I rejoice in the knowledge that you are becoming the whole-souled child of God, which at one time I feared you would never be. Remember, E. dear, the old and solid admonition, "Say much to God, little to men." And do not argue on religion but pray much especially at Mass and Holy Communion. You never hear an intelligent man speaking against the principles of our Holy Faith. It is only the base who, in order to excuse their own folly, scoff at religion. Be careful, dear E., not to relax. For what is this short life without the practice of the knowledge and love of God?—Nothing. And, "What is it when all is told?"—We are here for a few short years and while passing along life's way, there comes a cross for me and a cross for you, but God in the end makes all things right. Work then, dear E., for that other and better life whither we are all hastening. How quickly is one forgotten! The old adage is quite true: "Out of sight, out of mind," and if we are safe with God, it matters little.

Most affectionately yours,

SR. M. PAUL.

---

Elmhurst, June 8, 1912.

My dear E.:

How are you? Well, I sincerely hope in soul and body. Our school closed last week and soon we go to dear Ursuline, Santa Rosa, for our annual retreat. This year has flown! When I left Santa Rosa last August, to remain in St. Helena one year, it seemed an age to look forward to three hundred and sixty-five days. But how they flew. All things material are fleeting, therefore, why should we worry?

Do you make a visit to the King of Kings daily?

I know that my dear child meets with days of joy and of sorrow. Such is life. But when we are strengthened to walk the journey of life by frequent Communion, all things sad become sweetly tuned to peaceful endurance.

As I have said, have stated times for going to Confession and Holy Communion and keep to that time, if possible. Regular and frequent Communion will work wonders in the life of my dear E., but regular Confession must go hand in hand with frequent Communion and remember:

> "When earth's fair flowers are shedding
> Their fragrance on our way,
> There is danger in the sunshine
> If we should cease to pray."

So, my dear, say one decade at least of your Rosary every day. May God's blessing always be with you. "The heart of man is changeable and it can never rest till it rest in God." How true! You so tire of all the glitter that this world can produce and you reach for something that will live beyond the grave. Keep reaching and you will surely grasp it.

With fond love, I am always, dear E.,

Yours most affectionately,

SISTER M. PAUL.